My Angry
Breast

RUCHI ANANDA

BALBOA.
PRESS

A DIVISION OF HAY HOUSE

Balboa Press books may be ordered through booksellers or by contacting:

Balboa Press
A Division of Hay House
1663 Liberty Drive
Bloomington, IN 47403
www.balboapress.com.au
1 (877) 407-4847

Interior Images by Sharni from Shar Rose Creative.
Cover Image painted by RUCHI ANANDA

Print information available on the last page.

ISBN: 978-1-5043-0991-2 (sc)
ISBN: 978-1-5043-0992-9 (e)

Balboa Press rev. date: 10/06/2017

To Poppy

And to those who also leave behind threads of light
to be taken up by the
children of the future who will
have the wisdom, knowledge
and know-how to weave a new
blanket of light, love and peace

Contents

PART I THE CHEMO/TURMERIC DANCE

Tells the tale of my personal journey through the diagnosis, chemotherapy, mastectomy and the aftermath.

PART II THE CURE TO CANCER
IS PREVENTION

This section contains information on what I consider to be contributory factors towards today's cancer epidemic, information on natural medicine and lifestyle changes that can assist to find that holistic diamond of wellness. It is for educational purposes only and not medical advice. Cancer is serious and it is vital to consult qualified practitioners.

PART III SAY GOODBYE TO CANCER

PART IV BOOKS, DOCUMENTARIES AND WEBSITES THAT MAY BE OF INTEREST

Author's Gratitude

*"Sometimes our light goes out but is blown again into a flame
by an encounter with another human being. Each of us owes the
deepest thanks to those who have rekindled this inner light."*

(Albert Schweitzer 1875-1965)

My gratitude to the wonderful crew in my vision boat. I pulled
together the best for a bumpy ride and together we showed that
it can be done. True healing, true medicine is alive and well.

My gratitude to the doctors, scientists, health care workers and
writers whose work I have brought into my book. Holding a light in the
dark is not an easy task.

My gratitude goes to:

Friends who accompanied me on my highway of hope and have
been there every step of the way, a gift for which I am truly grateful.
For those whose stories brought wisdom and inspiration behind many
written words and those who sprinkle drops of wisdom from a higher
place. Friendship is a sacred link and when coming from the heart can
never be broken.

Friends whose love has survived a lifetime of memories that could
never have been imagined. Someone said to me that these friends are gold
and how true that is. How blessed I am to have had you with me during
those young times and to know that you are still here to walk together
through the years of silver and gold.

My precious Ganesh. You were an abandoned damaged kitten when

I found you but what a gift you were that I had no inkling of at the time. I will always miss you but hold within my heart the years shared.

Amber who I know will be bringing as much joy in cat heaven as you did whilst travelling on Earth.

I feel blessed for having experienced the sisterhood, women who have worn many garbs, felt the wind blowing in their hair and the sun shining on their face. Women who have survived many trials and still, one appears at your side when your world is cold and you are alone. I thank you from my heart dear sisters.

To Marni for being there every step of the way and the gift of a special spiritual family.

The jewel in the crown, my precious children and grandchildren. My 'Boys' who made it all possible but always have in more ways than you will ever know. My daughter-in-law for bringing a heart light to shine in those dark family recesses. As the picture frame holding a photo of the twins says, "Grandchildren are gifts from above to cherish and love," and to all my precious little earth angels I say, "Thank you for making my heart sing," and for giving an amazing reason to live.

To pre-readers for the wonderful editing suggestions.

To the proof reader for an amazing job.

To Sharni whose artistic gifts have brought a touch of magic with the visual of My Vision Boat.

To Carissa for your support and the photo taken of *Nanna's Rose*.

To the Balboa Press team for your support, patience and expertise.

Author's Note

Cancer first touched my life when I was seven years old with the passing of my maternal grandmother. Years later, I stepped the cancer highway with my beloved dad and in the year 2012, it revisited. This time the fear of the unknown was not so raw, having spent many years researching and studying holistic health I had an understanding of avenues to explore besides the toxic treatments offered by the Western medical model. When hearing those words, "You have cancer," I took the highway of hope to find a better way and a return to health.

With the guidance of family, friends and practitioners, I came to remember that there is value in all things and the Buddhist way of finding the middle road became a 'walk-your-talk' situation. Adopting an integrative approach, I walked a part of the allopathic medical way supported by natural medicine to find a quality prolonging of my life. During this process, I came to the realisation that the journey is different for each person. The alchemy of body chemistry, belief system, hopes, dreams and the cancer are as individual as each grain of sand on a beach. The therapies we bring together to support our healing also differ, especially today as I believe the modern medical paradigm is morphing into a holistic approach. I feel privileged to be a witness to this new emerging vision, one that is drawing threads from the brilliance of today's medical and scientific sector and ancient tried and true medicine whose heart beats with the mantra, "First, do no harm."

There are many wonderful books written on cancer, however, a heartfelt connection can only truly be made when sharing the experience of the journey. *My Angry Breast* has this quality, written from the heart, having heard those words, "You have cancer" and can combine this with resource information that can take months or years to pull together. When sitting in the doctor's office with a prognosis ringing in fearful ears, there is not that time.

This is based on a true story however, in respect for the privacy of others, names have been changed.

I give you knowledge gained from my journey that it may in some small way assist when travelling your personal highway of hope. It is a way strewn with tears, yes laughter and ongoing hard work but when my time comes to walk into the silence of tomorrow, my wish is for those I loved to remember that I lived well with cancer.

PART ONE
The Chemo/Turmeric Dance

What I call the Chemo/Turmeric Dance tells the story of my personal journey through the diagnosis, chemotherapy, mastectomy and the aftermath. It begins with my dad's cancer experience which is where my own thirst for knowledge to find a better way began. Pumpkin seeds, grape juice and hands-on healing were what I came up with at that time. However, today there is a wealth of practitioners with expertise in integrative therapies and this section tells the tale of how I put together what was best for my belief system, resources and cancer.

What Is Cancer

What is cancer
From where does it come
Is it a name given to that which beats a different drum
Does it play in the landscapes of creation
Seeking acceptance to become a different vibration
Is it a part of myself holding the rejection and tears
Is it the dark shadow's manifested fears
Is it a part of myself isolated and alone
Seeking a return to the light
To feast on the banquet of plenty and delight
What is cancer
From where did it come
Is it a name given to that which beats a different drum
Perhaps it is the cell that can change your life
Take you to new heights
Prompt you to let go of your silly ideas
Held for a lifetime from conditioning and fears
Perhaps it says, I am cancer
I am that what I am
And I too dance in the landscapes of creation
Even though I beat a different drum.

(Ruchi Ananda, 2013)

CHAPTER 1

You Have Cancer

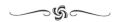

My heart wept watching the gaunt figure clutch the wooden stick. I knew the determination it took to climb the steep concrete slope to the car and tried to smile when he handed me a bright coloured box tied with a red bow. "Had to get you a chocolate egg for Easter," he wheezed through his pain. It was Good Friday Eve of the year 1977, a memory I will always carry telling of the love given by the man I was blessed to call my dad, affectionately known as Poppy. We had spent a long day at the hospital and when stopping at the local shopping centre on our way home, I left Poppy to doze, having no expectation of returning to find the car empty.

"The bad news is, you have cancer in the spine and the good news is, it can't get worse than this," the nurse had told him.

At the tender age of thirty-two I had no understanding of how the words, "You have cancer," would impact our lives. Weekends and school holidays became our only respite from the daily pilgrimage to the hospital, leaving early in the morning and arriving home at dusk and lasting for a period in excess of twelve months. I remember the doctors' frantic endeavours, clutching moments of hope and the times of prayer. When closing my eyes, I can see the emancipated bodies and the frozen fear in the sunken eyes of our daily companions, those human caricatures in wheelchairs and hospital beds. I can still taste the bitter rebellion and recall the quiet acceptance that this had become our everyday reality.

Poppy graciously acknowledged the bowls of pumpkin seeds and glasses of grape juice left beside his bed where they remained untouched due to the cruel side effects. Today, we have a smorgasbord of natural medicine practitioners to assist with side effects but in the 1970's this was not the case. Nor was there a wealth of written and cyber information to be found on diet, health and healing. Western medicine was the new panacea. Knowledge of the healing properties of plants, the body's inherent ability to heal and the wisdom of ancient medicine had dimmed in modern-day consciousness.

Despite having little relief from agonising pain, Poppy did not complain but said, "I've had a good life."

My brother commented, "Poppy showed us how to live."

I replied, "He showed us how to die."

I can always remember having an interest in natural therapies, perhaps inspired by family stories telling of my nanna's gift for healing and her knowledge of the medicinal properties of plants. One story I loved to hear was the time I lay dying in a hospital crib, diarrhoea being the cause. The doctors had shaken their heads and said, "No hope, sorry." However, Nanna came to the rescue making an arduous daily journey by public transport, carrying a precious brew consisting of the white of a newly laid egg and one teaspoon of brandy. I remember her selfless acts of love as being a sort of touchstone and smile when I catch a glimpse of Nanna in a grandchild's word, gesture or deed.

My own searching for that healing magic led to yoga, introduced to the West as a form of exercise that I embraced with enthusiasm. It was through yoga I met Joshua, a spiritual healer using the transference of energy via a channel in human form. Although this was forgotten knowledge in the world I lived as a child, Poppy agreed to have regular healings from Joshua. These helped with pain management but it was many years before I came to understand the importance of those healings in preparing him to leave the body. Western medicine has knowledge of the physical, our vehicle for exploring this Earth, but the dance of soul and spirit is hardly known or understood.

Poppy was our rock and the thought of him not seeing his grandchildren grow was heart breaking. There was no-one to witness my emotional turmoil and I had no idea that we were not walking the pathway to recovery. It was many years before I came to an understanding of the use of radiotherapy for relieving metastasis bone pain. However, after Poppy had passed over, Joshua revealed my dad's knowing that cancer was the vehicle for saying farewell to a life well lived.

The seasons of our lives come and go. Winter had passed for my dad but on the anniversary of his funeral, spring blossomed for me with the birth of my youngest child, Cleveland. I remember Joshua's knowing smile when looking at this precious babe and my belief that it conveyed the message that all is in Divine order. The wheel of life turned and in the year 2012, I too was faced with a diagnosis of cancer and treatments such as chemotherapy, radiotherapy and surgery. During those intervening years, however, I had passionately delved into many facets of the diamond of holistic health to gain knowledge that was to become a platform from which to begin the journey into the autumn of my life. All those years ago, the words, "You have cancer" changed everything and now were to do so again. This time, however, I had the leading role in a drama that would change my whole way of being.

Chapter 2

Following in Poppy's Footsteps

The sun was warm and the sky a vibrant blue the day I swum in the healing waters of a local creek. I had no inkling of the dark cloud waiting to eclipse until returning home and stepping out of the shower to see myself reflected in a large mirror. It was not the lumps, bumps and saggy skin that triggered a cold chill but a difference in the size of my breasts and a slight indent on the smaller breast.

I believed that I had sufficiently healed from riding the never-ending roller coaster of heartache and pain during the years of supporting my daughter, Lily, through mental health issues. I was eager to begin a new life. However, I knew my life was to take another twist the day I heard the doctor's words, "Have you thought about the therapies you'd consider if the diagnosis is cancer?"

Articles written in local magazines in the 1990's were my introduction to the doctor who was to steer my ship through the coming ordeal. Today her clinic offers integrative holistic health care bringing together alternative and conventional pathways to regain health. At the beginning of the year 2012 that is where I found myself, presenting with what is known as a peau d'orange.

"That's an angry breast," she sighed.

With those words, I stepped into the world of Western medicine and on my next visit, following the necessary tests, I was given a diagnosis of an attenuating mass highly indicative of a malignant neoplasm.

I wonder to this day at my calm acceptance that cancer had re-visited my life. I did not rant at God as I had done all those years before when hearing Poppy's diagnosis, but went to that quiet place within. My main concern was for those who were close and in this I believe, I followed in Poppy's footsteps. I also wonder whether that long year witnessing my dad's journey to his final breath-taking had prepared me in a way I little understood. Years spent studying and working with holistic therapies such as yoga played a part, as did learning to still the mind and connect with the spirit within. I remember Mary, a yoga student from long ago, her terminal cancer journey and her quiet dignity when being carried to class each week until leaving home for her final stay in hospital. When visiting, she told me that she only had to close her eyes for the rickety bed and cold room to be transformed into a place where the warm sun caressed her tired body. Mary said that yoga had prepared her for this time. I remember visiting another yoga student in hospital who refused major operations and everything that pathway, if chosen, would have brought to her final months. She said, "Yoga prepared me for my dying."

My doctor honoured my belief system and my decision to walk the pathway of natural medicine, however, there was always a 'but' until it was time to face another major cross-roads of choice. Those 'buts' saved my life.

"But, first I'll send you to a naturopath," she said.

The naturopath who was also an oncology nurse with one foot in the Western medicine camp and the other in the realms of natural medicine, walked the middle road. I was later told that these practitioners had known the Western way would mean chemotherapy, surgery and radiotherapy. They were to support in assisting me to make an informed decision, suspecting my life's experiences had led to a one-sided view.

Discussing my diagnosis with a former practitioner and friend, he said it was his belief that with my present doctor, I would make it.

If my doctor had lacked holistic awareness, I might not have made it. If she had not had the foresight to send me to a practitioner who could provide the knowledge and expertise to look with clarity at all options, I might not have made it. It was her belief that it is the right of the patient to have the final say in their treatment and this enabled me to feel supported at all times. Her comment to my daughter-in-law was, "The decision is Ruchi's … every woman's journey is different." A lot has to do with where your doctor points and in fact, your life will most likely depend on it.

I believe it is also important to have consulting and treating doctors who have an awareness of therapies outside of their own sphere of practice. If a doctor's knowledge is limited to the physical body, then the choices open to the patient are perhaps limited. Those specialising in Western medicine are taught this system with emphasis on the knowledge of drug prescription and the wisdom passed down from ancient physicians is little considered. It is a bit like sending a dress to the drycleaners and the decision is to decide which chemical to use for the best results. We are far more than our physical body, we are beings comprising body, mind, soul and spirit and dis-ease is an imbalance in our energy system due to many contributing factors. A return to balance can only be achieved by bringing together a potpourri of healing therapies to suite the individual's biochemical makeup, disease and belief system.

I did not believe my treatment options were confined to chemotherapy, radiotherapy and surgery. I believe in quality of life over quantity and although the prognosis indicated that my quality of life would be for a short period of time without taking the chemotherapy highway, I knew what I was doing, or so I thought. After completing the necessary legal documentation, the making of a Will, the Power of Attorney and an Advanced Health Directive (see Chapter 14) my next step was to make an appointment to see the acupuncturist. With his guidance, I would begin what I called, 'the carrot juice therapy'.

CHAPTER 3

Mustn't Say, "Never"

I met my acupuncturist in 2008 to experience what was described to me as his magical healing needles. Regular acupuncture treatments from that time onwards were an important part of my healing as he listened before offering insight into the emotional, mental or spiritual dilemma contributing to imbalance in my physical body. I always left with an 'Ah ha' moment.

One of his little gems was the story of the baby Buddha. At the time, I was recovering from years of stress with a lack of energy for the more physical pursuits. I arrived for a treatment feeling exhausted in anticipation of the yoga classes I was thinking of restarting. When telling him of my intention, he said that in some eastern countries those going through a similar healing process were often referred to as a 'baby Buddha'. Spending time in an ashram or monastery before re-entering the physical world of hustle and bustle was considered important.

Lying on the massage table with needles carefully placed on strategic points specific for my own healing, I drifted to another place of consciousness. An hour seemed like five minutes and when the needles were removed and my acupuncturist asked what I was thinking, I replied that I wanted to be a 'baby Buddha'. He said to go into the monastery and close the door. In my imagination, I did just that and my body responded with a sigh of relief. When I enter my inner sanctuary for a period of stillness, I can still touch the experience of that time in my life.

Acupuncture is a safe effective health care based on a coherent and substantial body of knowledge developed over thousands of years of clinical practice and intellectual study. Meridians, the basis of this therapy, are described in ancient literature such as the Huang Di Nei Jing (the Yellow Emperor's Inner Classic) the oldest and most revered Chinese medical text. The meridians can be likened to a network of highways transporting around the body the breath of life, called Qi in China, prana in India and Ki in Japan. Just as an accident occurring on a highway can stop the flow of traffic, lifestyle stressors can block this energy from flowing along the meridians, resulting in disease. Using needles, the acupuncturist can release the blocked energy allowing it to freely flow just as there are specialised people who clear the highway.

Acupuncture is a holistic approach, looking at the underlying cause of disease, the state of health, presenting symptoms and can assist in the prevention of disease as well as the maintenance of health. Treatment varies for each person and from appointment to appointment. Recent studies show that acupuncture has a positive effect on chemotherapy-induced nausea and vomiting, post-operative nausea and vomiting and post-operative pain (McDonald and Janz, 2017). Stress reduction and immunity enhancement are supported by a qualified practitioner offering sterile needles, alleviating the possibility of infection.

The day I saw my acupuncturist, armed with the initial diagnosis, I entered the clinic to be greeted by his partner, tinkling water, ambient music and an atmosphere of tranquillity. These practitioners have created this oasis to assist the art of healing and I was offered their valuable support by picking up the telephone and calling them at any time.

Cancer had entered my life and I was confident I was taking the first step on my healing journey. I was right, but not in the way I thought, my acupuncturist listened, reflected back the situation regarding my health, intended treatment and possible outcomes. I do not remember what was said, but the impact of his words sent familiar shivers throughout my body, a signal to pay attention. I questioned his experience with cancer patients and he replied that from his research and experience, the one common denominator regarding a successful outcome was belief in the chosen therapies. He said, "I'll walk with you whatever way you choose, but ..." The 'but' was the suggestion that it would be a good idea to have further tests to find out what we were dealing with.

My next step was to make an appointment to see the naturopath who also took a firm stand saying an informed decision could not be made until the completion of the necessary tests. Sidestepping the idea of following the anticipated 'carrot juice therapy', she said, "I'll walk with you whatever your choice, but, first we need to do a needle biopsy."

"Eeeeeek!" I said.

I was given a live blood analysis and supplements including turmeric, a cancer fighting and preventative herb. If I chose Western medical treatment together with natural remedies, I was assured that side effects could be alleviated. In hindsight, I came to the realisation that this practitioner had prepared me physically, emotionally and mentally for what lay ahead. Her knowledge of the Western cancer treatment model was important as she had an understanding of my expressed horror of poisoning the body and honouring my beliefs, fears and tears, she gave me hope.

I came to understand how vital it is to have practitioners with the knowledge and wisdom to support patients to safely navigate the labyrinth facing anyone given a cancer diagnosis. I also came to realise how essential it is for practitioners to work together. For instance, as chemotherapy has its own time of working, supplements must be given prior to and after this treatment so as not to interfere with the process. The acupuncturist also needs to be aware of the best time for treatment depending on the patient's response. An example is the story of a woman who had terminal cancer and spent her time between treatments in recovery with little quality of life. However, when having acupuncture before and after chemotherapy, she had fewer side effects, was up and about to her doctor's amazement and her family's delight.

The day I saw the naturopath, I drove through a red light and was to ponder on whether this was a sign indicating that I needed to stop and gain further insight before embarking on this journey. Chemo and turmeric are unlikely partners but I was to learn that in life and death situations can come together as a force to be reckoned with. It is a hellish dance like no other but perhaps a reflection of the Tao where yin and yang become a completed whole. Yin therapies were as natural to me as breathing. I knew how to relax, meditate, visualise, work with gentle yoga practices, eat wholesome organic food, be in nature and pray. I had barely dipped my toe into the yang world of Western medicine but I listened to my inner guidance and trusted the naturopath's judgement. An appointment was made to have the needle biopsy and my daughter-in-law, Deb, was there to see me through this ordeal.

Words saying, "We must never say, 'Never' when saving life is the issue," were later spoken by my doctor of natural medicine.

CHAPTER 4

The Diagnosis

I remember the evening of Poppy's diagnosis; the metal hospital bed, the white, sanitised room and my dad, a quiet man who only spoke when he had something to say. On this occasion, he said nothing. Not so my mum who talked incessantly and this night being no different, her voice filled the room and the empty spaces between thoughts, saying little despite the fact that there was a great deal to say. My brother's face was drawn, his wife unusually quiet. Silent tears formed a lump in my throat blocking that raw primal cry aching to be heard.

Nothing important was said, cancer was not mentioned, nor the proposed treatment. My mum's voice went on and on until Poppy's boss, Chen, entered the room. "I'm not here for you," he told my dad, "I've come for you to help me."

We left to give them time together. When thinking of that moment, I can still see the sadness etched on my dad's face and the hunched shoulders of the man sitting beside him. We will never know if they talked about cancer or the recent suicide of Chen's son, however, when Poppy passed over Chen said, "He's now caring for my boy." That was how it was, Poppy looking out for those he loved, his disease not discussed and the treatment, left in the hands of the medical profession.

The evening of my initial diagnosis was a different story.

I was feeling blessed when my sons, Cleveland and Aron and daughter-in-law, Deb, conspired to work together to give support, accompany me to practitioner appointments and when having tests. Sipping a glass of red wine in the comfortable surrounds of Deb and Cleveland's home, I outlined how I proposed to handle the new twist my life had taken. "The natural therapy path is the go," I announced to my family. They said, "Okay." However, their eyes told a different story.

Cancer is not something to tackle alone. Although Deb had a full-time job caring for twins under the age of twelve months, her mum was there to take on that task the day I was to have the biopsy and whenever Deb took me to an appointment. A gift was the time I spent with my daughter-in-law getting to know her in a way that would not have been possible through everyday interaction. Deb's gracious weaving of threads from an open heart intertwined with the love from my boys to become a firm foundation for the journey I was to take.

Aron was with me the day I received the results of the needle biopsy; a malignant invasive lobular carcinoma with one affected lymph node. We had a beautiful lunch and I spent that night with him and his partner, Marie, talking about life and dying. We laughed and we cried.

Close friends came forward offering love and support. "I can't get my head around this, but I do know I'm not ready to part with you," said Lee. "I'll miss our chats and cups of tea, but we can never be parted. It's more important to me to not see you suffer like my grandmother did," Mina told me. "I'm not ready to lose you," said Vanessa. "Every step you take along the cobbled path, I'll be beside you until we reach the pot of gold," my sister-in-law wrote.

When my doctor said, "*But* ... first, I'll send you to a physician for another opinion," I looked into my daughter-in-law's eyes glistening with hope, nodded and was given an appointment for that afternoon. I was to come to realise that in a short space of a couple of weeks, my practitioners had prepared me to take this step into unchartered waters, to know that my boat was sturdy, the crew shaping up to be the best for my situation and belief system.

Chemotherapy was the offered treatment and I declined, knowing it was wisdom to have as much information as I could gather before taking such a major step. My prognosis was not good and once again I looked into the eyes of my family and agreed to the next step, a bone scan, CAT scan and breast MRI. I had an understanding of the dyes, chemicals and radiation my body was to endure but believing an inner guidance had brought me to this moment, I followed that prompting.

The day I was to be given the tests, I reluctantly followed Deb into the waiting room where people sat erect, holding ex-rays. Televisions flashed the latest horror stories I rarely watched knowing the negative impact of those talking screens on the body, mind and emotions. We exchanged light banter and a few giggles surrounded by eyes not seeing beyond their personal world. I felt sad when looking into those hollow faces, sensing the chaos and despair.

My name was called. I was taken to a small cubicle from which I emerged dressed in a blue gown and white cap, horrified to see a cup of elixir being placed in my hand by an efficient nurse.

"Pretend it's a glass of red wine." Deb tried to smile.

Eeeeeeeeek!

"No-one dies on my watch," I heard my daughter-in-law whisper.

I had the bone scan, CAT scan, an MRI and my body purged the poisons. It was not until days later when seeing my acupuncturist that I again felt well. If I have those diagnostic tests in the future, I now know the wisdom of complementary treatment to assist the body to deal with this onslaught.

The day I looked into Deb's eyes welling with tears when the results reported no other cancer, I came to understand how my choices were affecting those close. After years of taking natural supplements and eating organic food, my general health was good. My doctor said, "Your blood tests are lovely, but that damn breast!" and that summed it up. Chemotherapy was the offered Western medical way. The mass had to be reduced before an operation was possible and chemo can be good at doing just that.

I believe food is a basic key to health. Following my initial diagnosis, I immediately eliminated anything from my diet that was not organic and locally grown or produced where possible. Replacing the glass of red wine, cheese and biscuits, happy hour consisted of a turmeric tea made from a recipe given to my acupuncturist by one of his clients (see Chapter 27). Processed sugar, known to feed cancer, was removed from my diet and meat consumption consisted of small amounts of organic chicken for making soup. I ate fresh local fish when available, juiced living food, drank chemical free water and organic teas. The change was not drastic as this is how I love to eat.

A dear friend, Mina, scheduled me into her busy life for a regular Reiki treatment, a technique to bring about inner calm and wellbeing. Reiki, meaning 'universal life force', is a means whereby this energy is transmitted through the hands of a practitioner, slowing down the brain waves to a meditational state of consciousness. Benefits can include relief from emotional stress and an increase in oxygen that will give the body a boost as cancer cells cannot survive in a well oxygenated environment. Mina also offered a cup of tea and a chat, so important at any time, but more so when living through a crisis.

Quantum science has shown that how we feel about what happens to us has an effect upon what we experience. Gregg Braden (2008, p 39) says, "The act of us simply looking at our world - projecting the feelings and beliefs that we have as we focus our awareness on the particles that the universe is made of - changes those particles while we're looking." While healing and illness may be happening at the same time, we will feel that healing is dominant if this is where we focus our belief. Therefore, our inner most intent is important to the outcome of our healing which takes place in a calm environment and therapies such as Reiki can take us to this relaxed state.

I listened to travellers, companions and bystanders on the chemotherapy path, but still could not agree to the treatment. Three decades ago, Poppy had left our lives having undergone Western therapies and little has changed as the offered treatment was, and still is, chemotherapy, radiation and surgery. Techniques are more refined and advanced but the side effects are just as devastating to those suffering and watching. With the internet at my fingertips, I delved into the mountain of knowledge available on the subject of cancer.

I discovered that monies raised for cancer research is usually directed into clinical trials. Controlled experiments using cell cultures, animals and humans are carried out to determine whether a substance, usually an artificial chemical, is safe and has therapeutic value. I have heard it said that for every ailment nature has a cure and whenever nature makes a mistake, she fixes it. Practitioners through the ages have used natural substances and a large proportion of the world's population still use natural medicine. Modern medicine took another pathway and today, doctors using natural medicine can be persecuted and closed down in courts.

One doctor who has endured this experience is Dr Stanislaw Burzynski, an internationally recognised medical doctor and biochemist who has devoted his life to cancer research. He is known for discovering a group of peptides, he called antineoplastons, that are part of our immune system and can act as molecular switches to turn off cancer cells. The movies of his story tell how he won the largest legal battle against the Food and Drug Administration (FDA) in American history and how his safe gene targeted cancer medicines discovered in the 1970's, completed Phase II FDA supervised clinical trials in 2009 (www.burzynskimovie. com). In the June of 2014, the Burzynski Clinic issued a press release to say that Phase III clinical trials have been given the green light to go ahead.

When antineoplastons are approved, it will be the first time in history a single scientist, not a pharmaceutical company, will hold the exclusive patent and distribution rights on a medical breakthrough with life-saving implications. Dr Burzynski's antineoplaston therapy has clinical data to show long-term recovery from some of the most incurable forms of terminal cancer, including brain tumours, pancreatic cancer and non-Hodgkin's lymphoma. For years Dr Burzynski has endured FDA attempts to suppress this knowledge and in the year 2016, this is still ongoing.

Dr Nicholas Gonzalez is another example of a doctor whose work with nutritional approaches to cancer treatment was undermined. His nutritional-enzyme therapy, after twenty-eight years of research and case studies showing results not to be found in the files of conventional medicine, was granted funding for clinical study in 1998. Dr Gonzalez's book, *What Went Wrong: The Truth Behind the Clinical Trials of the Enzyme Treatment for Cancer*, tells how his work was undermined. It won a Silver Award in the 2013 Independent Book Publishers Association Benjamin Franklin Awards - science category.

Many herbs and vegetables have cancer healing and fighting properties but little of the monies raised for research are channelled into this avenue of possibility. Dr Max Gerson, having healed his own migraines with a safe natural treatment, used this knowledge to put together a successful protocol for healing illness, including cancer. What is known as the Pepper-Neely anticancer proposal, was put to the United States Senate in the year 1946 to provide one hundred million dollars in funding for new cancer research if anyone could offer hope of a cancer treatment. Dr Gerson presented five of his cured patients, supported by five additional case studies before the Pepper-Neely anticancer subcommittee of the Senate Committee on Foreign Relations of the Seventy-Ninth Congress. The bill was defeated by the efforts of lobbyists working with four senators who were medical doctors (Gerson and Walker, 2006, pp xix, xxi). Vegetables could not be patented. Dr Gerson was prevented from publishing in peer-reviewed journals and continued to be harassed by the medical establishment until his death in 1959. Today, his daughter, Charlotte Gerson who is ninety-two years old at the time of writing, is successfully promoting his work through the Gerson Institute in San Diego.

I read about those who had healed and others who had not. Believing each step taken had come from an inner guidance, I waited for the next prompting but not without mental and emotional turmoil. There is enormous strength in the sisterhood and I was blessed when soft hands wove a blanket made from threads of love, compassion and enduring support. Kay wove threads into my beautiful etheric blanket. It was she who pointed to the path I was to take, telling me about a doctor who had brought a woman she knew through the chemotherapy journey to a place of wellness. "What about another opinion?"

Something deep within resonated with her suggestion and the following morning after a night of deliberation, I picked up the telephone. I was told there was nothing available for two weeks, however, a cancellation had just been received but it was for half an hour's time. I took this to be a sign and armed with ex-rays, reports and hope was there to meet this doctor who put together a satisfactory picture of my overall health. The exception was the information contained in the ex-rays he carefully scrutinised. When seeing a look in his eyes reflecting my doctor's words, I thought *That damn angry breast.*

I heard his soft, spoken words, "In six months, we might be saying, there's nothing further we can do." There it was, no 'buts' and in that instant, I knew my next step. This doctor who was also a practitioner of natural medicine, outlined the complementary treatments he could offer.

My doctor said, "In my thirty something years of practice, you've now brought together the best team I've seen for attaining many years of good health."

CHAPTER 5

The Drip that Kills

Good Friday Eve, thirty-five years from when Poppy had struggled up that steep slope carrying a chocolate egg, Cleveland and I walked through doors illustrated with palm trees, blue water and cerulean skies dotted with white clouds. Our introduction to the Oncology Unit of a local hospital was a receptionist who said, "Welcome to Fiji."

"I'm not okay with this," I whispered.

"Nobody is!" Cleveland tried to think of something positive to say and gently steered me to where a smiling nurse was beckoning.

The chairs were comfortable, the cubicle was private and Cleveland headed to the coffee shop leaving me to read the notes I was given on side effects that may occur. However, I was confident the complementary treatments I had undertaken would successfully support my body to endure the chemical onslaught.

"Are you ready?" the oncology nurse asked.

Never, I thought and put on a smile.

The needle slipped into the back of my left hand.

Drip, drip.

I pictured a beautiful golden healing elixir flowing into the cells of my body and then remembered my acupuncturist's words, "Think of it like draino getting rid of the old muck!"

Drip, drip, drip.

A baby Buddha does not watch poison slowly dripping into veins, flowing into organs, hands, toes and hair follicles.

Drip, drip, drip, drip.

"Sorry body," I whispered and thought *Chemicals are dripped into our food and water supplies, they saturate the earth we walk on and the air we breathe. Our bodies rebel, for no longer do they play in the sunshine and run barefoot on the earth. Our bodies rebel, becoming tired and stiff from living in an artificial world of chemical madness, raucous music, cruel lighting and invisible rays that zap at every twist and turn.*

Drip, drip, drip, drip, drip.

Cleveland returned. I thought *No child should ever watch his mother being slowly poisoned whilst hoping those lethal drops attack the cells gone mad. No child should ever watch the slow drip into his mother's veins whilst hoping the poisons miraculously bypass cells vibrating with life's dance. This is the drip that kills life and perhaps the mass of debris that has accumulated from a lifetime of living.*

I tried to smile when seeing Cleveland's eyes glistening with pain. We chatted, the minutes slipped into hours and then it was over.

Cleveland took me home to where two small children were waiting, he was thirty-two, the same age as I when all those years ago, I had taken Poppy home to where two small children waited for our return. A kinesiologist offered support through her potpourri of healing therapies. The session I had with her before commencing chemotherapy indicated that my present-day cancer had seeded at the time of the passing over of my maternal grandmother. She had been diagnosed with cancer and nursed at home by my mum who was thirty-two years old and had two small children.

I remember as though it were yesterday sitting on Poppy's knee and hearing that my beloved grandmother was no longer with us. I hear my mother's story echoing through the years, telling that nothing could be done for my grandmother and telling of the extra tablets given by the doctor to bring an end to the agony. That moment in time changed everything and as a consequence, my mum suffered agoraphobia for six years. Losing two of the most important figures in my young life in different ways would have been difficult to understand. My young heart hurt and it is possible that the pain remained energetically trapped in my breast, the place of nurturing, close to the heart.

Holistic physician, lecturer and author, Dr Bradley Nelson (2007, pp 64,71) writes, "I often find that trapped emotions lodge in an area that's vulnerable because of a genetic susceptibility, an injury or nutritional deficiency that weakens or imbalances the energy of the body in that area." He believes that over time, due to the imbalance of energy and irritation to the tissues of the body in that area, change may occur leading to a disease state and says that every cancer patient he has treated was found to have trapped emotions embedded in the malignant tissues. Releasing the trapped emotion which may have been a key player in birthing the cancer can give the edge needed to heal, support treatments and cause no future damage.

As a child, I went to sleep with visions of the adventures of Tinkerbell and the fairy folk, told by my grandmother. I loved that other world and after she was gone I searched for the little people, made moss gardens and left them treats.

When having follow-up kinesiology, I was taken to the seed event found in the previous session to when my grandmother had passed over. Unaware of the childhood connection to my grandmother and her magical bedtime tales, this lady gave me a book of fairy stories. I pondered on the thought that perhaps this was a sign saying I was healing a wound sown a long time ago, watered by life's tears and fertilised with beliefs, conditioning and fears. Gregg Braden (2009, p 139) explores this concept saying, "An experience carrying a strong emotional imprint at one time in life can become the primer for the conditions of that experience to repeat throughout other times."

When reaching the age of thirty-two, perhaps the cellular memory of my childhood pain was triggered with the passing of my dad and the loss of my unborn child. Am I experiencing this cycle again? If so, how will it play out and what can I do to change the outcome? Braden (2009, p 140) believes that if we know our individual cycles and how they work, they can become powerful allies in healing some of the greatest hurts of our personal lives.

Perhaps dying is not the issue but the healing of deep inner wounds that may bring peace to the heart and wholeness to the soul. Only then do we not leave a legacy of fear and pain, but one of love with an understanding that light and dark coexist, vying for attention and when acknowledged become an integrated whole, bringing balance. Trapped isolated emotions, like drops of water finding their way to the ocean, are then welcomed back into the sea of energy in which we swim, laugh, cry and dance. Broken bits of pain, locked in dark places and causing havoc in our lives are once again free, their story told.

*   *   *

A cancer given gift was to spend time with Chantelle and Dru, Deb and Cleveland's delightful twins. Their curious eyes followed my every move, sprinkling sunshine into the dark world of chemotherapy. In the weeks to come, they would squeal with delight when pulling off the head covering I was wearing to reveal my bald head. I yearned to snatch a cuddle, perhaps a kiss or two but my body was now toxic and precautions had to be taken. I could only watch from a distance the antics of these little ones, waking each morning to explore a room filled with beeping, whistling and singing toys.

My temperature had to be checked at regular intervals as a fever of 38 degrees C or higher could be life-threatening, meaning a speedy trip to the nearest hospital. The day following the chemotherapy treatment, I awoke on a high to be told this was because of the medication I had been given.

"What have I been missing?" I wanted to know.

However, the chemical effects wore off and I departed the land of the living to exist in a fog which was like turning off the beautiful coloured vistas of modern television, reverting to a bland black and white experience. I was sad and weepy coming down from the drugs designed to boost my spirits but knew that the doctor had mindfully put together medication to increase immunity, support my emotional wellbeing and to lessen side effects. I was saddened to hear of a neighbour who was not given this support and suffered terribly until being made aware that he could be helped in this way.

To minimise the possibility of thrombosis, a threat to chemotherapy patients, Cleveland accompanied my short daily walks bringing back memories of when he was a babe in a pram, my children, Lily and Aron and a German Shepherd called Hans. Whilst carrying Cleveland, I spent seven months with my feet up due to the risk of miscarriage. During this time, Hans rarely left my side, loved me unconditionally and soothed my sorrowing heart for the dad who had recently left our lives. Patterns repeat, my mum retreated into her agoraphobic cave and had little contact.

When Cleveland was born, our world changed. My heart ached the day I watched my faithful dog bobbing up and down in the back of the small truck taking him to a new home. Fear for the children's safety had to be the number one consideration as his jealous snapping and nipping was a real concern. I like to think it was Hans' time to romp on acres of land and my time to leave the dark world of grieving to embrace the wonders of new motherhood.

Although this once-upon-a-time tale is but a memory, its storyline was to replay. I was preparing to return home when a telephone call came from a friend suggesting it would be unwise to return to my loved eighteen-year-old cat, Amber. She had become fragile and I had been aware for some time that she was preparing to pass over. Uncharacteristic of this loving creature, she would attack at the slightest noise or movement, inflicting scratches and nips. I was reminded of the dangers of suffering an infection while undergoing chemotherapy.

"This is an accident waiting to happen," he said.

I remembered a friend's experience when breaking a finger nail whilst undergoing chemotherapy and the near fatal infection resulting from this seemingly insignificant event.

Amber was quiet when Cleveland slipped her into a carry basket. I held her when she closed her beautiful golden eyes and believed that she willingly sacrificed the remaining weeks or months she may have had to live. Cleveland, Deb and I wrapped her in green silk and buried her in my backyard overlooking the peaceful bushland.

"I'm not doing this ... back to the carrot juice therapy," I told Cleveland.

"Okay, Mum," he said.

"Definitely back to the carrot juice therapy," I told him the night I looked at my bluish, misshapen, quasi motto hands, as I called them. The funny thing was, at the time I thought *May-be they always look like this and I haven't noticed!*

This is known as peripheral neuropathy and can be a side effect of some cancer treatments, occurring when there is damage to the peripheral nervous system. It mainly affects the hands and feet with symptoms such as pain, weakness, numbness, tingling, loss of balance, clumsiness or dizziness. This may take time to repair once treatment has finished. "At least twelve months," an oncology nurse said. Natural supplementation was to help with this and when having future chemotherapy treatments, my hands were placed in cold gloves in an attempt to stop the chemicals reaching that part of the body. It is important to seek advice if symptoms occur as serious effects such as an increase in blood pressure or organ failure may occur.

On day seven, Deb drove me to an appointment with the doctor of natural medicine and my introduction to a new world of healing began.

Chapter 6

Losing my Mane

Tears dripped. My doctor of natural medicine who was also an acupuncturist, strategically placed a couple of needles and just like turning off a tap, they stopped. He carried out a live blood analysis before making me comfortable to receive intravenous vitamin C. At the same time, I had bioresonance therapy to assist with boosting the circulatory, lymphatic and immune systems. When toxic substances such as infections, chemicals and heavy metals enter the body these change its natural frequency which can result in disease. The body will always strive to detoxify these foreign substances and bioresonance therapy can assist the process by clearing blockages in the natural flow of energy. It is a non-intrusive treatment that has been used in Europe for over thirty years.

Chemotherapy kills white blood cells, an important part of the body's defence for fighting disease. I agreed to have this treatment knowing I would be quickly replenishing and rebuilding from the toxic attack to the body. The acupuncturist, also worked on detoxing, boosting immunity and helping to correct emotional, mental and physical imbalances. The naturopath prepared my body for chemotherapy and gave me extra confidence to keep walking this cobbled pathway. She said the first treatment would be a blueprint for those to follow, enabling complementary treatments to be better gauged. The difference to my wellbeing before and after receiving these treatments was remarkable.

I went home to my loving cat, Ganesh and flowers from my friend,

Kay. Flowers are one of my favourite things and she woke on a regular basis to fossick in her acreage garden, putting together a bouquet of colour and went to sleep every night with her mobile phone and a track suit handy. If my temperature went up, I only had to ring and Kay would have been there to whizz me to the hospital before an ambulance had time to pull into the driveway.

Someone asked who cared for me and when I replied, "My old cat," she said, "But, a cat can't make you a cup of tea when you don't feel like getting it yourself." I did not suffer nausea, vomiting, diarrhoea or constipation, lived in a rural environment and had an abundance of fresh organic food and purified water. I was surrounded by help if needed and although Ganesh could not put the kettle on, she was always nearby, giving love and comfort, asking little in return.

A heartfelt disappointment was not being able to celebrate the twins turning one-year-old. The big issue at the time was the danger of infection, however, I had come to realise just how depleted my body had become. Chemotherapy was birthed out of World War II research when it was discovered that toxic poisonous nerve gas used in chemical warfare was lethal to rapidly dividing cells, which includes cancer cells. It is highly toxic and has an effect on the whole body including bone marrow cells. These are instrumental in forming the white blood cells that are crucial for fighting infections. The long-term effects include the poisoning of vital organs and cell mutations that can lead to the growth of aggressive cancers that are difficult to treat.

Nights alone were scary. Being winter, my Hinterland home was cold, especially so with a depleted body fighting for survival and I kept my warm cosy combustion heater alight twenty-four hours, every day. Boxes of kindling and logs weathered by nature's hand for long burning were delivered and this precious bounty was lugged up a steep flight of stairs to stack on the verandah close to the back door. Although I wore gloves when handling the wood, I still managed to get a splinter in one of my hands and this tiny break in the skin, normally a job for my immune system, could not be dismissed. The possibility of infection hung like a shadow over my shoulder and I rang the oncology department of the hospital to be told it had to be removed as soon as possible. A neighbour found me on her doorstep and heard, "Can you get a splinter out for me ... or I'll die!"

She did and I did not die!

Be careful what you wish for. Many years ago, I remember saying to my hairdresser, "Think I'll go bald!" When he shook his head, answering with an emphatic "No!" I knew my vision of a smooth, shiny, bald head to complete the "monkish-look" when wearing my chaddha (a robe used when meditating, symbolic of going within and withdrawing from the physical world) and taking yoga classes was not to be.

My present hairdresser, has been a wonderful support from the moment I sat in the chair casually saying, "Of course, I'm doing the carrot juice therapy." The scissors stopped and after a long moment, he spoke about clients and their cancer journeys. Everyone I entrusted with my impending decision indicated that Western therapies needed serious consideration.

My falling hair was gradual and although I ignored those wispy clumps gathering on the polished wooden floor, the day came when I could no longer do so. I popped in to see my hairdresser and jokingly said, "What are you going to do with this?"

Inspecting the thinning locks, he replied, "This is where you're going ... now!" He was adamant that I visit the wig shop immediately and I was grateful for his foresight, knowing I would need a wig sooner than later. He was to comment that to be on your own and to have your hair fall out can be a soul-destroying experience but to be prepared may make all the difference. How right he was.

Being a Leo lady, my mane is important. When my hair began to go white at a young age, regular visits to a hairdresser were a priority. I now ponder on the thought that through the use of hair dyes, I had subjected myself to toxins containing carcinogenic chemicals that can end up in every organ and cell. Professor Samuel Epstein (2013, p 25), a leading authority on the causes and prevention of cancer, includes 'dark hair dyes with early and prolonged use' in his list of avoidable causes of breast cancer. Many years ago, when gaining an awareness into this toxicity, I had searched and found a hairdresser using safer plant-based products. However, chemical dyes were now no longer a concern, Wynona, the name Deb had given to my wig, would not grow roots to be touched up with colour. Wynona suited me perfectly, being a similar style to the way I had worn my hair, but my scalp was extremely sensitive and my bald head in no way resembled the 'monkish-look' I had envisaged years before.

The first time I wore Wynona was when my friend, Lee, took me to an appointment and then for coffee. We were sipping and chatting when she looked aghast and said, "You can't do that!"

"What?"

Sitting in a busy coffee lounge, I was lifting Wynona and scratching my scalp! Nor did I remember to pay for the coffee when Lee slipped into a nearby shop. Chemo brain was also a new experience. 'Chemo brain' or 'chemo fog' is the term coined for the effects from some treatments and can result in memory problems, difficulty in concentrating, confusion, fogginess, or fatigue. This is officially called post-chemotherapy cognitive impairment (PCCI) or sometimes referred to as mild cognitive impairment (MCI). Good nutrition can assist to repair the damage that can last for years.

Lee graciously returned another day to pay the bill.

CHAPTER 7

Pointing the Bone

Tears flowed from Aron's eyes on occasions since my diagnosis. I had encouraged my boys to express emotion and not be afraid to share those precious watery drops of love, sadness and hope. He cried when we were driving to his home on that fateful day. His eyes grew misty when we entered 'Fiji' for my second chemotherapy treatment to receive a warm welcome, not from beautiful Fijians but women in nurses' attire armed with needles and toxic drips.

Wynona was not yet comfortable to wear. The first thing I did after settling into a cubicle was to rummage through a basket of scarves made by a local lady for those enduring the chemotherapy experience. Aron bought three and a nurse lovingly arranged a mottled white and brown scarf to cover the wispy bits of blonde fuzz. "You look beautiful," she said, admiring her handiwork. With Aron's generosity and the nurse's gentle compassion, I could almost believe I was shopping in a resort.

Aron went in search of coffee and a needle slipped into my arm.

Drip, drip.

I thought of a friend who had an adverse reaction to the chemotherapy dripping into her veins. How terrifying it must have been when her body froze and she was not able to breathe until saved by her mum's quick reaction and a nurse running. After recovering from this ordeal, her oncologist decided to 'give it another try'. When the same response nearly claimed her life a second time, how brave my friend was to trust that another chemical concoction would not create a repeat ordeal.

Drip, drip, drip.

I said to my friend, Anna, "I don't dream ... chemo has taken away my dreaming."

She replied that it did and when first experiencing chemotherapy said her youngest son dreamt her dreams, giving her messages received. I missed my dreaming and the connection to my spirit self, now fuzzy and far away. A darkness that was foreign to my nature had entered my being and flowed through my blood to every cell in my body. I pondered on the thought that Aron and Cleveland were like sentinels guarding the doorway to my diminished awareness and dropped a tear that my daughter, Lily, was far away.

Aron's success in life, his swimming career and reaching high rungs of the corporate ladder at a young age grew from an innate determination to succeed. He had expressed the belief that if he could succeed with the challenges in front of him, he would be doing it for Lily who would someday return to adorn us with her talent, beauty and personality. However, we have come to accept that our world is nothing like the envisioned fairy tale, dreamt so long ago. Life happens and we have to keep keeping on. Aron is now dreaming a new dream but for a moment in time, like Cleveland, has made space in a busy schedule to support the transition to another phase of my life. When the time is right, I will resume my dreaming and create a new dream. I do not know what that will be but I do know I have to keep keeping on.

Drip, drip, drip, drip.

The 'pointing of the bone' is documented in aboriginal lore and perhaps by today's medical profession. A diagnosis is made and when the harsh chemical treatments fail, the bone is pointed and more often than not, becomes a self-fulfilling prophecy. The 'nocebo' effect is a well-known medical term, meaning the interpretation a patient makes when receiving a fateful diagnosis. If the doctor's attitudes and beliefs surrounding a diagnosis are negative, then the patient can be left in despair and without hope. New research indicates that a cancer diagnosis may be as fatal as the cancer itself, dramatically increasing the risk of suicide and heart-related death following the diagnosis (Fang et al., 2012).

Harald's introduction to the scary world of prostate cancer began when he underwent a test to check his blood for the level of the prostate-specific antigen (PSA), a protein produced by the cells of the prostate gland. Receiving a high reading, he found himself in a specialist's office listening to a proposed treatment plan conjuring images of his manhood under threat and a waning vision for a healthy future. No compassionate glance or word came with the prescribed therapy he had the foresight to write down. It was business as usual for this doctor. Upon returning home, Harald checked the recommended procedure to discover that it came with a long list of possible debilitating effects to health and wellbeing. He knew there was another way and rang the specialist's office to cancel the next appointment. Within minutes, Harald received a return call from the doctor who said, "In my opinion you're riddled with bone cancer and you'll die in agony in two years if you don't do what I have prescribed for you." The bone had been pointed and Harald's heart shattered. This ancient form of dark magic had caste its spell coming from a place one would least expect, a modern-day Western medical specialist. Perhaps Harald would say he did die a death in the days and weeks to follow waiting for test results and suffering a dark depression. When the results came back saying that no cancer was present in his body, Harald set about researching and putting together a plan to reduce the risk of prostate cancer occurring. Perhaps a gift from that soul shattering incidence is that he is now supporting his healthy lifestyle with natural therapies and is experiencing a deeper reverence for life. To this day, Harald wonders how a PSA reading could have invoked such a dire response and is aware that although it is an important detection tool, it does not conclusively indicate that cancer is present. What if he had believed what was told to him and hopped onto the medical merry-go-round?

Another of my acupuncturist's gems puts it nicely when he says there are spiritual belief systems often giving an ultimatum, "It's my way or the highway ... only through me can you climb that stairway to heaven."

Modern medicine can at times work with a similar concept, "It's my way or the highway ... only through me can you heal."

Drip, drip, drip, drip, drip.

Dr Deepak Chopra (2006, p 54) describes the human body-mind as part of a conscious thinking field of intelligence. He says, "The average person thinks about sixty thousand thoughts a day. This is not surprising. But, it's a little disconcerting that 95 percent of the thoughts we have today are the same ones we had yesterday. Every day we unconsciously create the same energy patterns that give rise to the same physical expression of the body." When receiving a prognosis for a dismal future and a limited time to live, what if we had the realisation that this is only one choice of belief? What if we replaced it with an optimistic outlook supported by lifestyle changes such as introducing a whole-food, plant-based diet, reducing stress, creating a chemical free environment and including life-sustaining complementary treatments?

Cancer perhaps is the number one fear in our modern world and it has been predicted that by 2020 everyone may experience cancer at some time in their lives, whether personally or through a loved-one. Why? It is my belief that lifestyle is a major key. It is said that if we keep on doing what we have always done, we will always get what we have always got. Cancer is a destination. I hopped on a train a long time ago with the best intentions, the courage to survive life's challenges and arrived at the present station. Do I remain on the same train or change to a completely different ride? I believe the answer to these questions came with research and soul searching, that is taking the time to quiet the mind to allow my inner wisdom to have a voice.

As a child, I lived in an area surrounded by vegetable gardens. I believe knowledge of today's chemical pesticides, herbicides, insecticides and artificial fertilisers had not yet reached the ears of the local farmers peddling their produce door to door. However, when first married, we lived in a rural area with commercial vegetable gardens close by and from that time until leaving the area, I suffered mysterious allergic reactions. I believed that I was buying the best food choices for my family from the road side stalls supplying freshly picked produce. Chemical sprays were definitely used with abundance at that time but sadly, I had no awareness of the consequences to health and the environment. Today, there is a wealth of information and scientific studies to correlate the growing incidence of disease and the introduction of modern farming methods.

When moving to a new home in the 1990's, I have memories of waking in the early hours of the morning to peer out of the window to see a fine white mist being sprayed from a Council truck. Those pesky mosquitoes would have been zapped and everything from plants to humans. Years later, I became ill when a house I was living in was sprayed for white ants and some years after that episode, I broke a lease to leave under similar circumstances.

Perhaps, the weakened part of my body most susceptible to my childhood pain had over time suffered further damage from everyday living, such as environmental poisons and lifestyle choices. Perhaps cancer is a cry for help saying change is needed and fast.

Drip, drip, drip, drip, drip, drip.

When the last drop had entered my vein, the needle had been removed and my second chemotherapy treatment was complete, Aron escorted me to his comfortable car. During the long trip to his home I wondered what he was thinking behind the smiles and bits of humour bringing laughter to this theatre of horror. The little boy playing within his heart space and protected by the man he had become flashed an occasional grin, reminding me of love received. Perhaps when the final curtain is drawn, the boos and the applause fade into the silence and our time on the stage of life is done, this is what remains to say we once danced and sang here.

When driving through a newly constructed tunnel, Aron asked if I was okay with this as he had an understanding that I was not always comfortable with confined spaces. I wondered whether this thoughtful man, whom I still think of as 'my boy', had memories of looking after his Poppy so long ago. Up until the age of approximately seven years, a child's experiences recorded in subconscious memory become a foundation for the emerging belief system. Four-year-old Aron loved to sit on Poppy's knee and was involved in the day to day care of his grandfather. I wonder whether his interpretation of that experience has played a part in enabling him to cope today.

I later welcomed questions from Aron's son, Bray. "Do you have cancer?" - "Are you going to die?" Hopefully, I gave him answers to support a positive learning around these important issues.

I kept notes for my practitioners and my thoughts on the improvement from the first chemotherapy treatment.

- *Support team in place, now kicking in and working fantastic.*
- *For my journey at this time, physical, emotional, mental and spiritual support has been gifted to me.*
- *Trust in my practitioners.*
- *Acceptance towards the chemical treatment and a decision to use this to my advantage as I know that any effects experienced can be minimised.*
- *A Reiki session the day prior to treatment.*

I was prompted to create a 'Vision Boat'.

My Vision Boat

A Long Healthy Life Free from Cancer

Helm
General Practitioner

Doctor of Natural Medicine

Naturopath   Acupuncturist
Reiki Practitioner Kinesiologist

Rudder
Family - Friends
(Love and Support)

Supported by: Organic Diet, Supplementation, Vegetable
Juicing, Meditation, Relaxation, Yoga, Rest, Visualisation,
Positive Thinking, Earthing, Heliotherapy, Walking, Holistic
Dentistry, Massage Therapy, a skilful and caring Phlebotomist.

A friend who was in regular contact, joked, "Are they giving you lolly water?" He sees blood test results during the course of his work and understands the devastating effects chemotherapy has on the body. Blood counts can drop to a dangerous low, an indication that the immune system is badly compromised. Patients can then be put into hospital to be given a blood transfusion in order to be able to have yet another dose of chemotherapy. I was holding my own and put it down to the complementary treatment. To my way of thinking, it is imperative to prepare the body before and after treatment and to rebuild as quickly as possible before receiving another onslaught. Clinics and hospitals in Germany and Europe offer complementary therapies such as intravenous vitamin C as a matter of course. Low dose chemotherapy is often combined with the best complementary treatments, thereby minimising horrible effects that weaken and debilitate.

Fear can bring to pass what we fear, but perhaps my children's belief in the Western medical treatment I was undergoing had in some way counteracted my own fearful disbelief. I had faith in the complementary medicine I was using and with the support of practitioners, family and friends, the chemo/turmeric dance was taking on a life of its own. Awkward steps and movements were becoming co-ordinated, a blending into one rhythm, direction and goal.

CHAPTER 8

The Silent Witness

On the morning of the third round of chemotherapy, I took time to focus on visualisations to change any negative thought of the ordeal to come and to bring about a sense of a positive outcome. When Cleveland arrived, I was focusing on the time I would spend with him, Deb and the twins.

Before taking medication, I always source the pros and cons so as to be well informed, however, I did not do this with the chemotherapy I was given preferring not to place in my consciousness the side effects that could occur. The routine was now familiar and after settling into a comfortable cubicle, Cleveland headed to the coffee shop and the needle once again slipped into my arm.

Drip, drip, drip.

My mind went back to Christmas the previous year. I had been to a wedding and on the way home was driven into Sydney to spend time exploring before returning home. I had always wanted to see the life size terracotta warriors from Xian, China and there was a display at the Art Gallery that day. Michelangelo carved the famous statue of David out of stone and it is told it was his belief that he only had to chip away the excess stone to reveal what was there. Who, I wondered chipped away stone to reveal this colossal army and what did they experience in so doing?

I loved the men of stone, stoic in their determination to achieve what,

I do not know. Wrapped in earth, like Egyptian mummies embalmed for a future time, did they now revel in the crowds who 'oohed' and 'aahed' at their splendour? When travelling the world, would they see people coming from a place of heart having evolved to be the caretakers of this wondrous planet? What would be their thoughts when discovering that no part of the pristine world they once knew has escaped modern man's toxic contamination? What would they think seeing the man in the cubicle next to mine taking that slow drip? "If I'm here then," I heard him say to the nurse. What would they say if they knew that this experience was perhaps his last for this lifetime?

Drip, drip, drip, drip.

I loved the stone carriage and the horses, reminding me of the yoga teachings applying the metaphor of the carriage as the body. Pulling it are horses, representing the five senses, taking it whichever way, the reins symbolise the mind and the driver the intelligence. Inside is a passenger, the all-knowing silent witness, the one with the wisdom and knowledge to guide our vehicle to a higher perspective. I pondered on this thought and left the gallery to encounter another experience giving me cause to wonder.

Wandering through Sydney's famous Hyde Park, I spotted a delightful department store window displaying moving snowmen, carol singers and reindeers pulling Santa sitting in a sleigh filled with gifts. Lilting voices conveying messages of giving and loving reached the ears of the milling crowd. I spotted a young man dressed in rags and sitting on a small part of the concrete with his back against the window. Long scraggy hair hid his down-turned face and in front of him was a piece of hessian on which lay a sprinkling of coins. I stood to one side to become the silent witness.

No-one acknowledged the presence of this man sitting cross-legged like a yogi in contemplative meditation. He appeared to be invisible to every man, woman and child but I will never forget his clear blue eyes looking into mine when I placed a coin at his feet and heard the whispered words, "Bless you."

Drip, drip, drip, drip, drip.

It is my intention to do the best I can to become that silent witness in order to harness the power of the senses to steer the body along a pathway that will bring about fulfilment of my soul's purpose. I will falter, spend time peering into that black hole of despair, regret and blame, but there will be times when I will rejoice in receiving the gifts of life and for those special souls met along the way. One such occasion was the day I entered the clinic of the doctor of natural medicine to hear a voice say, "Hello Ruchi." I had met Thea some years before whilst undertaking emotional literacy training and enjoyed a friendship from the moment our eyes met. I was astonished that she had recognised me. Wynona did resemble my own hair but I had lost ten kilogrammes, the harsh treatments had stripped away so much and time had not yet rebuilt the new woman I was to become.

She said, "I recognised your smile. You've come to the best place ... it took me two years to find this doctor. As a matter of fact, if I had come here for treatment at the beginning of my journey, I believe my story would be a very different one today."

I was honoured to be sharing my journey with this courageous woman but my heart cried when learning about the cancer side of her life and meeting her boys standing on the threshold of manhood. Every week, one or the other embarked on the long arduous trip to take their precious mum for treatment, patiently waiting for hours before returning home to face another week of life's challenges.

We shared cherished moments, always leaving the clinic feeling replenished not only with the life-giving nourishment flowing through our veins but with hope in our hearts. One day, Thea confided in me, saying, "A gift from the cancer is that I can now feel emotion." Her eyes lit as she spoke, "I can now feel the good and the bad ... the joy, happiness, pain, fear. As a child, my heart closed, I couldn't feel, but now I can and that's exciting because I'm living. To experience it all is to be alive in the moment." From the beginning of her cancer journey, some eight years ago, Thea had searched for answers and found the courage to face her childhood pain. Her wisdom, acceptance of what is and a delight in life are her gifts to those who are willing to see.

I thought of the sightless people relishing the illusion of a moving window display, ignoring the human suffering at their feet. I wondered who our most profound teachers were and what it would take for humanity to wake from the dream created by modern day illusionists - the politicians, the media, the new gods and goddesses of film and television to name but a few? If and when it does, what will be the experience? Will it see that life is what it is, pain and suffering on one side of the coin, happiness and joy, the other? Perhaps it is only by feeling the emotion in the moment that we ever truly live.

Drip, drip, drip, drip, drip.

I left the clinic that day wondering, "What is the personal message cancer is delivering to me?"

CHAPTER 9

The Operation

Not even the familiar coffee lounge felt warm and inviting. Tears streamed down Aron's face and Cleveland's eyes glistened when he placed cups of coffee on the table. I wondered what a mother did in such a situation.

We had just received the results of an ultrasound taken after the third round of chemotherapy. The finding of an increase in the mass of tumour sitting in my right breast with evidence of a further mass-like structure was quite shocking. As was the thought that the chemotherapy was not working!

Eeeeeeeeek! I thought but when I said, "Back to the carrot juice therapy," the doctor replied, "Yes, Ruchi, *but* ..." The 'but,' was a letter of referral to a specialist for another opinion. I instinctively knew that I was in capable hands and my next step was revealed. My heart said that this was a change of direction as my body had taken enough chemotherapy, its job done in order to move onto the next process. A date was set for a full mastectomy, giving five weeks to rebuild my strength before facing a major operation.

My cancer has been described as the trickster. Invasive lobular breast cancer can be difficult to diagnose, does not always form a firm lump and is not always detected by mammograms. However, I trusted my inner guidance. I believed that my decisions regarding the treatment to date had come from this place, resulting in a calm acceptance of what is, free from the manic-depressive state that could have occurred. It goes back to the direction your general practitioner points as to how the dominos fall and now that trickster was to give up its secrets.

My doctor supported my decision, saying, "You look great."

"It's the wig and the make-up," I replied.

"That applies to us all!" she said with a grin.

It was Dr Emoto (2003, p 93) who said doctors should be philosophers as well as healers and believed that a doctor's deep insight and compassion could contribute towards a patient's healing process. This I believe is a key to my own journey from the time of the diagnosis, the chemotherapy and now the approaching operation. If any one of the practitioner crew in my boat sailing towards a safe harbour was without these valuable assets, I may not have continued along the chosen pathway but perhaps would have mutinied to a world of hope and promises. This was not the case, these practitioners combined have extensive knowledge of Western oncology treatments and natural medicine and they all have insight into the heart of the patient.

My body was now ravaged by chemotherapy and required specific treatments to prepare for the operation. I had preparatory work to do, talking to my breast and giving gratitude not only for what it had contributed to my life but for the sacrifice to be made. I knew that cutting out a chunk of body did not solve the problem. We are not bits and pieces but a whole unit and there are many factors to be addressed to bring about healing.

It was my acupuncturist's belief that over the past years I had done the hard work, the healing almost complete. Most people, he said, get a diagnosis and then go about finding their healing process, but I had done this in reverse. Healing the physical aspect of my disease or imbalance was now my job.

A friend asked, "What of my life's experiences was the most difficult?" I replied, "Those 'baby Buddha' years." She was surprised, saying I had hidden this well.

My cousin sent photos of angels to fly into my email box, to be printed and taken to every chemotherapy appointment. One day, she emailed to say she had come from a consultation with a psychic and had asked if there was anything in the reading regarding my health. The lady said she always picked up on chronic illness but in my case, could only sense a tremendous positivity and no cancer throughout my body. Perhaps this reinforced what my acupuncturist was saying and on other levels I had cleared the dis-ease. My cousin was told that the pathway I had chosen to date was the correct one and because we are close, this information could be given.

*   *   *

On the morning of the operation, Cleveland, Aron and myself entered a waiting room filled with people holding ex-rays and suitcases. A name was called and ever so quietly, someone disappeared through a solid wooden door guarded by a nurse who bestowed the same smile to all who entered.

Eeeeeeecck!

It was surreal to see all eyes glued to a large screen where brawny bodies chasing a ball received whoops and boos from animated spectators.

"This is insanity!" an inner voice said.

"Not wrong," another replied.

"Watching football could be the last thing we do!" the first voice said in disgust.

"Yeah, not my cup of tea … my dying wish would not be to watch football!"

I breathed, nodded at something Aron said but did not hear and was called to the desk where a receptionist thrust forms under my nose. "Just paperwork," she said. I completed these before returning to my chair to gawk at the flickering screen to see a large man with bulging eyes catch a little ball and hug it as though it were life itself.

"Silly game!" My inner critic was not giving up.

"This is a life and death moment, and we're watching football," my inner Venusian whimpered. "No make-up, no nail polish, no hair and NOW …," she complained.

"Escape?" my inner sleuth suggested.

I looked toward the door we had entered and stooped to pick up my bag to hear my name being called.

Eeeeeeeek!

"Don't let's walk through THAT door," was the inner command lost in tight hugs.

"We'll be waiting," my boys chanted.

"Never see them again!" my inner depressive announced when the door to the operating theatre complex closed behind me.

I thought, *Never again!*

After being poked, prodded, blood pressure taken, weight and height duly noted and my clothes placed into a large paper bag, I was guided to a mobile bed wearing a hospital gown, white paper pants and cap to match. A Florence Nightingale made gentle conversation and then disappeared leaving behind reassuring words.

The anaesthetist appeared brandishing a large needle. Visions of Aron and Cleveland floated before my eyes and voices chorused, "Never again!"

I dissolved into blackness.

I awoke to find myself surrounded by nurses, beeping equipment and bright lights. On the bumpy ride to my room in a squeaky bed I thought, *I'm definitely not in heaven.* This was confirmed when I found Aron and Cleveland waiting. Ooops, I made a mistake when trying to appear normal, attempted to eat the dinner proudly presented by a jolly woman. Somehow, I made it to the bathroom despite the attached cords, pain machine and drains slipping along the floor like puppies.

Waiting in my room was a lovely bunch of pink lilies. These reminded me of the time Poppy was in hospital and I took him a pink baby rose grown from a cutting taken from Nanna's garden. This was the only time it ever blossomed. When I visited the following day, he said, "They gathered around the rose last night." I enquired as to who 'they' were to be told, "Nanna, Pop and Bill." These were his deceased family.

My experience was different. I awoke one morning to 'see' a huge brown bear at the foot of the bed, my scream bringing every nurse in the ward running. I whispered, "I was dreaming!" However, Mina arrived with a cuddly bear her youngest boy, Ray, insisted on buying and a friend called, Ru, the following day with another to match. I called them Rayben and Ruben. These little mascots clung to me like glue for the whole of the hospital stay and now sit in my pink breast cushion as a reminder of the part given to gain much more. Sometimes when the loneliness descends like a mist, I reach for these little ones to be reminded of the enormous bear standing guard at the foot of my bed. When my grandson, Roger, arrived with a card on which he had drawn a bear, I knew the symbolism of the bear was important during this time of healing. Bears are prominent in the mythology of nearly every Native American tribe and are considered to be a medicine being with the strength and wisdom to heal their wounds.

I was fortunate to have a large private room and gave gratitude for the beeping technology, determined to accept whatever I needed in the way of Western medicine to bring about a speedy and successful recovery. The continuous intravenous antibiotics and blood clotting injections were lifesaving necessities. The room slowly transformed with the arrival of cards and flowers from which I created an indoor garden where I could sit and contemplate. After a couple of days, I could explore and discovered an outdoor area where fresh air, the warmth of the sun and walking on the earth could assist the healing process. I gave gratitude for food served with a smile, knowing that in a short time I would be able to resume meals prepared from fresh organically grown fruit and vegetables.

Visitors arrived on waves of love. Mina took me on my first outing to the coffee shop, those bags of drains draped over my arm like a handbag. She said, "I have photos of you smiling the day after your op."

There was nothing like hearing, "Hello Nanny!" and seeing a double pram entering the room carrying Chantelle and Dru.

The histology report came back reporting a grade one malignant invasive lobular carcinoma, two affected lymph nodes and clear margins. If such a report can be called good, it was on the side of being the best it could be.

I was fortunate that my hospital stay was slightly extended until the dreaded drains could be removed. However, it was not until the morning of my departure when stitches were removed that I glimpsed where my breast had been. Weeks later, I showed Deb the jellyfish replica of a breast I had just purchased and could only shake my head and say, "No," to her suggestion to give it a name. It remained in the box for many weeks, untouched and ignored.

I was accepting of what was, however, tears fell over what I knew were an accumulation of losses throughout my life. I would say, "My body's crying," as that is how it felt. My body cried and cried.

During the 'baby Buddha' years, I cried the tears I was not able to release throughout my life. When Lily said, "Cry for me, Mum ... I can't cry," my soul cried for her and for the children in this world who suffer. Lily said, "My heart is broken and can't be repaired." I had cried for the broken bits of heart floating around seeking to become whole. My body now cried for its recent loss and triggered that deep soul grief but no longer did I deny my feelings, acknowledging that they open the doorways to becoming whole.

Part of the 'baby Buddha' healing involved reclaiming the lost parts of myself given away to others or to events. It was a time of recluse, writing and purging. Facing the cancer, that large ball of lived life and releasing it in gratitude was perhaps a final stage in singing the bones of the 'old' woman.

Emerging from the ashes is a new woman in the process of becoming whole.

CHAPTER 10

An Oasis of Healing

Mother Mary, Gaia, Pachamama, the Sophia. Speaking these names brings a reverence to the heart, a longing to curl up in the sacred womb from which we emerge. Of all the archetypes, perhaps the 'mother' is the most longed after, our primal instinct is to return to the bosom of the mother in a time of crises.

I did just that and when leaving hospital, Cleveland drove me to a friend's beautiful home. Her garden oasis, watched over by a large statue of Quan Yin the Buddha of Compassion and Mercy, was the perfect place to capture drops of sun and to heal. The eyes of Buddha beheld the meditation room and my journey from sporting a bald head to a mop of frizzy hair to a gradual return to a short-cropped style. During the recuperation period, I had photos taken in front of the large Buddha painting, a record to say, "Yes, I was that but now I'm this." I like to think that the golden Buddha was smiling at the small but courageous steps I was taking.

Cocooned in this peaceful sanctuary, I could begin my healing process and close the door on a world I often see lacking warmth, nurturing and heart love. A world where the family unit has broken down, a sense of community is like a voice crying in the wilderness and people have lost touch with themselves, each other and the natural world to the extent that they have forgotten how to truly heal. However, true mothering heals everything, the ravished body, the chaotic mind, depleted emotions and can even recall bits of broken heart. Learning to do this for ourselves is vital to our wellbeing.

Psychologist and author, Dr Patricia Sherwood (2007, pp 9, 10) believes the Sophia, the personification of healing through wisdom, has been in exile from mainstream life for generations and her exile has broken the connection between body, mind and spirit. She says, "Human experience has been belittled by rational analysis. Alienated from our experience, human beings have increasingly sought meaning in fragmented and distorted realities: their bodies through consumerism and materialism, their minds through narcissism and hedonism, their spirits through addictions and cynicism. It is not surprising that fragmentation has spawned a growing epidemic of depression, suicide, anxiety and violent behavior." Dr Sherwood speaks of the Buddhist belief that developing compassion for others is the key to healing this societal malady we are dealing with today.

The outer world is but a reflection of our internal loss of personal peace, the result of a yang society split from its yin counterpart. The male qualities of strength, leadership and protection to name but a few, are distorted by many to become control, abuse and greed. The balancing female qualities of nurturing, caring, unconditional love and wisdom when suppressed, can give rise to self-rejection which in turn may lead to a judgmental attitude toward others.

Cancer seeds can incubate in broken hearts, loneliness, fatigue, stress and an inner yearning to live in an almost forgotten mindful and soulful way. It was Rudolf Steiner who said that cancer is a 'cold' disease. It can grow roots in the black holes within our energetic system that come from abuse, rejection, a lack of warmth and nurturing. These we attempt to fill with addictions. I remember my own mother turning a cold cheek instead of a warm hug and her old auntie always giving that cold cheek. When subjected to a cold feminine heart in early childhood, fear and uncertainty may be the result and have negative lifelong consequences.

Perhaps an antidote to cancer is warmth, softness and gentle loving. Thinking about this prompted me to do a little housekeeping, to discard what no longer served me and to say farewell to those who were not truly supportive. I cannot heal another but I can heal myself by knowing that I am not a victim of disease, powerless to heal. As a matter of fact, I am the one responsible for my healing, having contributed to its causes through unwise and unaware lifestyle choices.

Lessening environmental stressors is important as it has been said that our body struggles to maintain health and vitality in today's toxic environment. Commercially grown food cultivated with poisonous chemicals and lacking nutrition may also be genetically modified, a process linked to serious health risks in studies carried out by a growing body of independent scientists. It has been estimated that there may be in the vicinity of eighty thousand man-made chemicals in use that were not with us in the 1940's and the majority of these are untested for carcinogenesis. Our bodies are subjected to electromagnetic frequencies and radiation of which there is no safe dosage, its effects are cumulative. Harmful chemicals and radioactive elements can join forces in a dance of death, each supporting the carcinogenic effect of the other.

Diet and lifestyle are fundamental to wellness, even though the Western medical model tends to ignore this well documented fact, just as it does natural medicine. There is a lot of research to say that organically grown food filled with the life-giving energy from the sun, rain and soil really is medicine. I believe that healing the immune system is the key, not treating symptoms and attempting to poison our way to wellness, a process causing so much damage that the scene is set for a more aggressive cancer to return that can be difficult to treat. Sunshine, sleep and laughter are strategies I incorporate into my plan for holistic health. I had to be careful of the amount of sunshine I was exposed to because of the chemotherapy however, I knew that would change. Vitamin D deficiency is well documented in the cancer story as is the need for quality sleep and the positive effects that laughter has on the body, mind and spirit.

Cancer thrives on fear which is used as a control mechanism by governments, religions, the media and sadly, a proportion of the medical profession. There is wisdom in the American Indian saying that we have two wolves inside of us, one good and one evil and the one we feed is the one that will win. Fear of cancer is well fed in the Western world. Fear turns 'on' our fight and flight system releasing powerful chemicals into the body to support the impending danger. However, when this system is not turned 'off' these same chemicals can seriously deplete the body, leading to adrenal fatigue that has been linked to many health disorders including the cancer story.

Negative emotions can undermine any treatment but it has been said cancer does not find it fun being in the body of a person who is not afraid of it and can depart. This may sound simplistic, but perhaps when a cancer diagnosis is given, working through the initial fears and setting the stage for a miracle is a good strategy. We do not know when our time on Earth will complete but whether living or dying with cancer, bringing positive resources into our day is a recipe for meaningful moments in time. When Cleveland returned to take me to his home, I left my friend feeling as though I had been wrapped in a warm and fuzzy etheric blanket.

Chemotherapy and a major operation had desecrated my body, held together by those of my crew with knowledge of natural medicine. I had not been given lolly water and although I was not completely aware of this at the time, I was severely depleted from therapies that had assisted in saving my life. It was not until months later when a neighbor said, "You've been very ill," that I really began to know this. When I asked, Lee said, "We were worried." Western medicine exposes patients to this cruel treatment with little, if any, supplementary healing support on the physical, mental, emotional or spiritual levels. However, with knowledge gleaned over the years and the support of practitioners, friends and family, I came through this ordeal with no setbacks.

The chemo/turmeric dance was giving an award-winning performance.

I do not remember much about my next round of doctors' visits except to glimpse a preview of the next step along that cobbled pathway - more chemotherapy, radiation and hormonal therapies. In my mind, I was prepared for more chemotherapy and some radiation but not to the extent I discovered it would be given with no room for negotiation. My fuzzy chemo brain needed time to consider the next step. For Western medicine, it was a given but because of the results, I believed other pathways were now open.

I was at another crossroads, but this time it was me using that powerful 'but' to put on the brakes and change the course of action. Vanessa was visiting from interstate and as she was not here to support, offered her time to take me to appointments. It was Vanessa, a highly skilled counsellor, who held that moment of decision with compassion and I will always be grateful for her love and wisdom in holding that space without personal input. Battering on the windows of my mind were the flapping wings of the beasts of fear. I heard the occasional, "What if?" and that giant thought form, fear, so much a part of the cancer model, loomed like a dark shadow of doom until the decision was final.

I was given statistics for my age, health, tumour type and results to date. Aron researched and when seeing the small window of hope, taking into consideration the possibility of years to recuperate from the treatments, said he knew my decision. Deb and Cleveland showed concern, however, on the night we gave it serious consideration as a family, humour was brought into the discussion. "Well, Mum, I'll keep you in my budget for another ten years," said Aron looking at the ten-year survival rates for those with my particular type of tumour. Without the financial support of these 'kids' as I called them, I would not have been able to have the complementary treatments vital to my ongoing wellbeing.

At the time of my original diagnosis if the cancer had spread to the rest of my body, I would have seriously considered natural medicine as my therapy of choice. However, with much deliberation I had come to understand that the way I had chosen was a good option. Because of my recent results, I now believed a different strategy could be considered. Our body makes everything needed to heal but cells released into the blood to zap the renegade cancer cells are sometimes overwhelmed and are 'taken out' by chemotherapy. Slow growing tumour cells may return more aggressive and difficult to treat. This is where I believe complementary therapies are important, in building up immunity, repairing damage as quickly as possible and supporting the body to keep renegade cells at bay.

If my results had been different, I do not know what pathway I would have taken but I do know the same deliberation would have been given to making a decision and to not be rushed into further treatment. I knew the beliefs, hopes and fears of family and friends who walked beside me with no pressure or input from personal fears as to what they thought I 'should' do. That is unconditional love. During this time of decision, the practitioners I worked with were able to do what Vanessa had done at that crucial moment, hold the space with wisdom and compassion. That is true medicine, but not all practitioners take this approach.

Natascha nursed her precious husband, Klaus, for five years with a diagnosis of stomach cancer. The tumour disappeared with chemotherapy and then he endured a major operation. When that 'cross roads time' happened and Klaus' inner guidance said "No", he rang the oncologist to say he was cancelling the appointment for the next round of chemotherapy. "You can't do that!" he was told. Klaus, being in a state of complete exhaustion, gave in to the doctor's persuasive undertones sending those beasts of fear into a frenzied flapping of wings. Chemotherapy kept Klaus alive for a time but at what cost?

Natascha goes to sleep at night thinking it could have been different. She often wakes to find her garden alive with flowers and believes this to be Klaus' reminder to her that there were other pathways of choice. However, the one they chose gave the gifts of people met along the way, nurses and doctors hoping the treatments given held the stuff of miracles. Lives touched for a brief moment that would otherwise, not have been possible.

Perhaps, he is saying that whatever the chosen way, smell the flowers, see the beauty of each day, the colour of a petal, a drop of moisture on a leaf as it is all too fleeting and the time will come when we walk into the silence of tomorrow.

Healing can only come from following our inner intuition and heartfelt guidance. The doctor of natural medicine said, "It's no good having vitamin C drips thinking you should be having chemotherapy." Whatever therapies chosen by the patient are right for that person at that time and that is when the greatest chance of success will be the result.

The dance of life and death I call the chemo/turmeric dance, bringing the yin and yang worlds of natural and orthodox medicine together had for a time spun into a frantic tango, the yang being predominant. A breath had been taken and it now glided into a slow waltz, the yin taking the lead with both partners in step.

CHAPTER 11

Releasing the Pain of Yesterday, Today and Tomorrow

Cleveland lit the fire and carried in supplies of food before leaving to return to his work-a-day world. However, I was not alone, surrounded by nature spirits I fancied peeped from behind every tree and plant.

Ganesh loves to be in nature, whether hail, rain or shine but remained close and cried that night, the first in my own home since leaving for hospital. I have heard that an animal can transmute the pain of its human family. I listened to my cat's deep mournful cry and I wondered.

A new grief touches and mingles with old grief that can be smouldering under a pile of daily living, like a mound of dry leaves waiting to ignite into a blazing flame. When triggered, this flame can engulf every cell in the body and erupt like a volcano to become uncontrolled bursts of anger. I did not release my anger in this way but have no doubt that it remained in my body as my doctor saw when she said, "That's an angry breast." I suspect, the ball of anger that had been physically released held the tears of years, the pain of yesterday, today and tomorrow.

Kay's mum said that I was like a little plant and in order to heal needed the same careful nurturing a plant requires to grow. The earth, air, water and fire elements vital to the growth of our plant kingdom are also important to our wellbeing. Included in what I call healing rituals are conscious contacts with the earth, breathing in air from the unpolluted area in which I live, soaking in water free from nasty chemicals and regular sun bathing. I now look back on those 'baby Buddha' years as a significant turning point in my journey and I believe the 'little plant' stage will also be a chapter in my book of life. Writing this, I am still a little plant in need of nurturing and will remember this truth, as I now know the value of retreat and how to create a place in my every day to stop and unwind.

Just as we go to a beauty parlour and emerge looking different, I was now physically not the same as when I had stepped onto this pathway. The chemicals and the learned expertise used by beauty therapists are not the ones oncologists and surgeons wield, yes, I had been given a makeover but one that would not wash or wear off in the near future. Whereas the pedicure or blow dry might make me feel uplifted for a time, my makeover was deeply ingrained. When I looked in the mirror, I saw someone I did not recognise. The little girl, the lovely teenager sparkling with hope, the young mother weaving dreams for her babes had blended to become a stranger. Be careful what you wish for, I was thin, too thin and thankful that I had carried extra weight, now gone.

I wondered, "Where do dreams go? Do they ever die?"

Lee sent a beautiful hand knitted scarf and hat. Mina wrapped me in scarves and the most delightful red beanie I wore thinking it looked like red hair. I still smile when remembering some youngsters comment, "Funky hair!" I chuckle when remembering a later comment, "Thank goodness you have hair and no longer wear that awful red beanie!" Writing this from the other side of chemotherapy and memories of a bald head, I treasure these lovely knits.

When my hair grew back white and curly, Mina's boy, Benny who had seen the wig, the bald-look, the bandanas and the beanies asked, "Is that your real hair?"

I instinctively replied, "No, my hair is ..."

Mina finished the sentence with a giggle, "Blonde out of a bottle."

The image I was not so long ago, was how I still thought of myself. It was no wonder the white haired 'old' lady did not compute with what I 'saw'. I was not an old, white-haired lady, but the change was sudden and permanent. I could go to my hairdresser and he would transform the white frizz into a lovely blonde, but I was not the inner person I had been a short time ago.

Mina said, "You've been fighting for your life." That changes you on a cellular and heart level.

Someone said that old friends are like gold and I know this to be true. I met Di in primary school, she hopped on an aeroplane and came to visit when I was staying with Deb and Cleveland after my operation. Later, Di was to say that she wanted to be with the 'old' Ruchi to chat and talk like old times, but it was not the same. Apart from suffering the effects of chemotherapy and the operation, I was now different and I understood how Di felt.

When Poppy was fighting for his life, I remember commenting that Poppy had already gone. I now realise how lonely it must have been for him with those around willing him to stay when he was preparing to leave. I see my own letting go through the personal cancer experience as a releasing of worn out masks. Yes, I have chosen to stay in my physical body for a longer time, but it is a bit like being one of those soldiers in a body of stone, embalmed for so long and then unearthed to find yourself in a different world. That is how I felt.

Part of my doctor of natural medicine's script for healing is to forgive. Not only did I need to detox the physical body but also the mental and emotional aspects of myself.

I know my subconscious mind does not differentiate from what is real and what is imaginary. Those programmes (beliefs), given by caretakers, society, religion and schooling can run the show. When I catch an 'old script' playing, such as, "I'm not loved," I use a tool like ho'oponopono, a Hawaiian forgiveness ritual (see Chapter 27) to erase the old memory. It goes back to having an awareness of thoughts that can be whisperings in my ear from a moment in past time. The little child wounded so long ago may still have a voice but when her fears are acknowledged, the old tape does not continue to play. The wounded child is no longer alone.

I have done a lot of work over past years releasing false beliefs taken into the subconscious and replayed on a conscious level when the correct buttons are pushed. However, I now believe it is time to forgive myself, accept myself and love myself. Perhaps that is all I ever needed to do to begin the process of integrating the light and the shadow within.

Forgiving others does not mean to condone evil deeds but to look with a soft eye through the wisdom of compassion. The unconscious will lash out when hurt, they hit, scream and stab in a desperate attempt to stop the pain. The unconscious will gossip and tell untrue tales. I now know that it is not only okay to distance myself from such toxic environments, it is mandatory to my healing.

Another part of this doctor's script is to have a vision for the future, something to aim for perhaps years down the track.

We are sent to school in our society to be trained to exist in a certain way, to become a doctor, solicitor, truck driver or an office worker. We may become a wife, husband, mother, father, sister, brother or friend but when chronic illness enters our lives those masks can fall away, our energy will then be directed to the art of survival. We are not taught the skills to deal with a situation we thought was for others but never us. The script we are handed is more often than not from a doctor following the Western model and can predict a future as being non-existent, the present, bleak. Finding meaning in what can seem to be a time of angst and despair is not a skill usually found in our box of tools.

Victor Frankl (2006) said there were many in the concentration camps who died not from lack of food and medicine but from lack of hope or something to live for. He believed that while everything external can be stripped away, the freedom to choose how we respond, feel and put into action about what happens cannot be taken from us.

Someone said to me, "Now I know, I'll never get cancer ... only the best people do." Perhaps cancer does feel more at home in a body that is good at giving rather than one that is continually taking. Perhaps a diagnosis is a sign that it is time to bring balance into our lives and to say no when a situation is not in our best interest. Every bit of energy is needed for self-nurturing and a return to wellness. I am learning to say no to those who insist on 'dumping' worn out dramas, like lifting the lid on a rubbish bin and pouring in unwanted baggage for safe keeping. It is time to take that rubbish dumped over the years to the tip.

When "NO" is said with feeling, intention and peace within the heart, it becomes a powerful force, a vehicle for the soul to smash those walls of illusion that are built over time. Our true nature is revealed when those tattered rags woven from threads of fear that cling to the human form are transformed into a glorious garment of light.

With the required financial resources when originally diagnosed, I would have seriously considered visiting one of the overseas clinics specialising in treating chronic, degenerative disease, cancer being one of the specialties. A place where every area of holistic health is addressed by highly specialised doctors and practitioners using cutting-edge technology. However, I believe that promptings from my inner guidance had led me to bring together one of the best teams offered in this country.

I am blessed to have therapies such as intravenous vitamin C and bioresonance technology in a place surrounded by the beauty and the peace of nature. This not only offers a valuable backdrop to treatments but can soften the fear experienced by those enduring harsh Western oncology therapies. In this clinic, patients chat, laugh and share stories in a cocoon of safety. A caring team encourage this vital interaction whilst ensuring every patient's wellbeing is supported at all times. Some like to sit in comfortable chairs with their feet up and chat while receiving that drip of life. I love to lie on a comfortable bed while drinking nature's beauty through large windows, knowing I am in a place where body, mind, emotions and spirit rest in stillness and peace. This is true healing.

Angelo Druda (2009, p 139), a traditional Chinese herbalist, said "Wherever there are examples of benign human community, there tend to be also pleasurable healing spaces and homes. A wise clinician knows how this works. The best healers and doctors always create a peaceful, living space in which to receive their clients. Such small healing sanctuaries can have as positive affect as the medicines and the treatments. Sometimes just being in such a space can heal people."

This is not always the case today and the welfare of patients who are depleted in energy is not always a priority. I was saddened to hear of a friend's experience with the public health system, oncology department, being too exhausted to ask questions vital to her wellbeing after waiting three hours to see a doctor she did not know. I remember the time I accompanied my daughter to see her doctor to find the reception area crammed with fearful people, waiting for anything up to two hours for perhaps a few minutes of the practitioner's time.

"It's okay, Mum, it's always like this," Lily had said.

Is it okay? I bit my lip, refraining from further conversation having learnt that I could not make it better for Lily as she had to choose her own way.

When I made my first choice to not follow Western medicine, my doctor said that at some stage the cancer would have to be faced but in the meantime, we did not know what could eventuate. That wise doctor had given me a platform from which to step onto the highway of hope. Perhaps another practitioner may have implied that I was doomed if I went down that pathway but instead, a seed of hope was planted and a safe place from which to begin my journey was created.

The wish for my wellbeing behind the words saying, "With your doctor, I believe you'll make it," spoken at the beginning of my journey came true.

My 'Vision Boat' is indeed sturdy, build with precision and has a crew providing skills for a safe passage.

CHAPTER 12

The Wisdom of Nouse

Little things matter and can make a difference.

A local handyman keeps my lawn neat and the surrounding area free from mounds of leaves continuously falling from overhanging trees. However, on the day he came after my return from hospital, he kept tidying and after washing the car, his keen eye sought jobs begging attention. "I've two strong hands ... you're not well and need help," he said.

Every week, a beautiful card arrived in the post from a long-time friend and Kay kept the house smelling of flowers. I arrived home from hospital with what I called my 'wave of love'. This consisted of cards I placed in one spot and breathed in the love they represented throughout the days of my recovery.

I keep a bookcase filled with photos, ornaments and bits and pieces that are a reminder of those I love and who love me. I send love to these people and breathe in the love I imagine flowing back. This is known as resourcing, a powerful tool to bring joy and strength into the body. That empty black hole in the pit of the stomach whirling with feelings of despair, hopelessness and abandonment can be immersed in qualities to support recovery. Hope may seem far away, 'out there' somewhere, but can be breathed into every cell in the body so that we can act, move, feel and think from a place of connectedness.

Each morning I greet the day and give gratitude for the many blessings received. To consciously relate to what is beautiful and good encourages the cells in our body to vibrate on a higher frequency. Resourcing can be sitting in a place in nature, or a favourite spot within your home, breathing in the colour of a beautiful flower, holding a loved-one's hand or listening to music playing the strings of the heart. Resourcing is a science known to ancient healers saying what we feel in our hearts, we make true in our physical world.

Stories of man's evolvement from poor living conditions, a short life span and little or no knowledge of the art of healing, support propaganda which is the foundation of a business machine called modern medicine. It is told that Hippocrates, known as the father of modern medicine believed in treating the whole person, not just the disease. Liz Simpson (2000) said that treatments such as massage with essential oils, hydrotherapy, fresh air, sunlight, exercise and wholesome food were found to be so effective, the philosopher Plato was known to complain that people were living too long.

The healing properties of medicinal plants were well documented at this time, however, with the introduction of organic chemistry around the eighteenth and nineteenth centuries, formulas were changed and the concept of high price marketing began. The knowledge of nature's inherent ability to heal became an almost forgotten art with the introduction of synthetically made drugs. Natural plant medicine could not be patented or generate large monetary profits. The oath of the true healer, "Do no harm," became a small voice crying in the wilderness of big business. Today, the pharmaceutical corporations that have evolved from this beginning are the voice behind what is taught in medical schools and the manufacturers of synthetic drugs backed by the scientific data produced by the same companies. They are also behind the propaganda we see daily on our television and the laws persecuting those brave scientists and doctors who beat a different drum.

Although the evolvement of trauma therapy and techniques in the field of surgery have given many blessings, the toxic pills, elixirs and oncology treatments of today will cause physicians of the future to shake their heads in sorrow. However, with a little 'nouse', we could combine ancient knowledge with modern science to leave our children and grandchildren a legacy to make our last breath a worthy completion.

Poppy taught by his everyday living, giving to others from a place within the heart where thoughts and actions are given due consideration, the consequences seen at the beginning of the race. Shaking his head, he would say, "There's no nouse," meaning there is little common sense. He believed all the book learning in the world was useless without a bit of nouse thrown in. This word recently caught my attention and I learnt that it represents the mind within the heart, the connection between soul and spirit, the wisdom we use to ride the waves whilst surfing in the great sea of life and the vision within the soul (Nahmad 2008, pp 67-69). By learning to go within, the natural breath can take us to a place of peace where the gift of nouse may be granted and we may find the inner physician who knows the true meaning of the words, "First, do no harm."

In Section Two I have listed some well-known integrative cancer clinics working with the concept of bringing together many facets of the diamond of healing to give each patient the best possible outcome. Practitioners willing to step outside the box have put into place a blueprint for a new dawning in the field of medicine. It is up to us, the patients, to demand the best that medicine has to offer be made available to all people. This, I envisage, is the future of oncology for the betterment of all concerned. In the meantime, putting together my own plan was the only option, to apply Poppy's nouse and to seek the inner physician to heal my body, weakened from the treatments and my mind, now fuzzy and forgetful. Heal thyself, as the saying goes.

I do not believe there is a magic pill to heal cancer and when putting together a 'recipe' for a return to wholeness, reconnecting with nature is one important ingredient to include. People have lived on this wondrous planet for eons of time with ears finely tuned to the earth's song, eyes to see the beauty of creation and the nouse to walk a soft journey and do no harm. Indigenous people understood that nature's supermarkets supplied food rich in life-giving nourishment and herbs to heal every ailment. Their homes featured carpets of healing earth in a variety of coloured grasses and ceilings dancing with stars, comets, moons and suns.

Western culture has lost this connection to the earth. As a consequence, shocks to the body, which are relentless in our modern-day living, are not transmuted through the natural earthing process. The breath may be blocked at the point of impact and perhaps in that moment, a cancer cell can be born, destined to survive with little need for the oxygen of life.

Dr med Ryke Geerd Hamer found through scientific research that there is a clear connection between the moment a shock or trauma happens and disease occurring in a particular tissue. Based on scientific data, Dr Hamer tells us that cancer is a natural biological emergency measure that has been in effect for millions of years and his dedication has given us the healing model of German New Medicine (GNM). According to GNM the time it takes to heal is the same as the trauma phase and therefore, it is important to deal with trauma as quickly as possible. Sadly, Dr Hamer passed over on 2nd July 2017, but his work will continue and can be viewed at www.learninggnm.com.

We cannot change a traumatic experience but through imagery and intention with the support of a body-mind practitioner, we can change the energetic cellular memory. For instance, I remember a kinesiologist telling the story of a young boy whose behaviour changed in a moment in time. From a well-balanced child, he became fearful, fretful and difficult to manage. Due to the practitioner's skilful use of kinesiology it was discovered that his mother had taken him into a supermarket, left him in the trolley and disappeared for an instant. The child thought he had been abandoned and the unexpected shock lodged in the body triggering behavioural changes. The trauma was resolved and the boy reverted to his calm, peaceful self.

My cat, Ganesh, spends a lot of time sleeping, lying in the sun and on the earth. Birds flutter nearby, but never a twitch of a muscle because long ago she adapted to rural living and to trusting that her needs would be met. I have adopted Ganesh's recipe for living into my healing programme and on a daily basis, weather permitting, have contact with the earth, breathe in the fresh mountain air and soak in the sun's healing rays. I am slowly healing from the shocks that are a part of the cancer journey, the diagnosis, the treatments and the aftermath.

My doctor of natural medicine tests the supplements I am taking on a regular basis to ensure they are needed at the present time. Even though a supplement may be excellent for fighting cancer, it does not mean it will work for your cancer, or agree with your body. We vibrate at different frequencies and so do the medicines we ingest. Our bodies fluctuate in frequency with different stages of healing and everyday living and therefore, it is wise to check supplementation on a regular basis. Ensuring those pills and elixirs work in harmony is important.

One pill does not fit all. Every person is different as is every cancer and therefore supplementation varies from patient to patient. Blood tests are valuable in determining what is needed. In my case, vitamin D and selenium levels were depleted and these are two vital strategies to have at maximum levels to tackle cancer cells. This is where your integrative/ naturopathic practitioner comes in and just as it is important to have 'cancer doctors', 'cancer naturopaths' are a must. That is, therapists with experience in working with cancer and an understanding that this is a life-changing process.

Tests to detect cancer at an early stage and give information on what supplements, herbs and food nutrients are likely to work are now available (see Part Four - Genostics Testing). I believe it is a wonderful first step in putting together a plan of action and can alleviate the hit and miss approach. Tests to give information on what chemotherapy treatments are likely to be more suitable are also a wise choice. Conventional blood marker tests are not always accurate, diagnostic tests such as CT (computed tomography) and PET (positron emission tomography) scans give the body a dose of radiation as do mammograms that are not always accurate. Ultrasounds may not be accurately read and when a biopsy is performed on a cancerous growth it is said the likelihood of it spreading and triggering inflammation is high. Western medical diagnostic testing can be life-saving and necessary, however, becoming informed as to the choices available and making decisions around personal resources are important.

My belief is that nutrition is the cornerstone to any treatment and is a continual work in process. I eat locally grown, freshly picked organic produce and this is made possible because of where I live and my determination every week to make the trip to a weekly organic market. Another one of my favourite things is the greeting received here from the smell of real food, a smorgasbord of herbs and a choice of breakfast delights. I can feel the difference when walking into a place where the genuine happy smiles of pride for produce grown with love is the reception. This is in contrast to supermarkets filled with products pumped with chemicals to appear freshly harvested and being confronted with marketing signs created to entice you to buy. These I rarely visit as I believe it is important to support local businesses for without these, our choices will be sadly diminished.

Community is the glue here and people such as these, working together for the benefit of all, are the pioneers of a new emerging frontier. I have heard it said that there are no new challenges, mountains to climb, nor rivers to swim but I do not believe this to be true. As we expand our minds, new frontiers will appear. Projects such as integrative medicine, green chemistry and farming methods designed to produce life-giving healthy foods will bring challenges because the results we are seeing from the 'old' methods are calling for better ways.

These markets are the work of farmers who beat a different drum and believe that worldwide food shortages will only get worse. We need to produce locally grown food to not only become self-sufficient but for a long and healthy life. Geoff Buckley (2008, p 13) pointed out: "The world has an epidemic of health problems with increasing rates of cancer, obesity, diabetes, heart problems, Alzheimer's, Parkinson's, ADD and so on. Nutrient-rich food without herbicides and pesticides is the solution, but nearly all the world's research is focused on finding patentable drugs to sell to help alleviate the symptoms. There is finally a reluctant acceptance that if you eat organic food you will live long and in better health." Bev Buckley (2010) tells us that organic farming according to nature can overcome problems related to the changing climatic conditions, because healthy plants have a strong immune system and can survive and flourish. We are of the earth and so can we.

Perhaps, cancer's voice is saying that it is time to become aware of why we are suffering ill health on a scale never before seen.

Like any plant that has been given a dose of poison, I now needed careful recuperation to restore my former vitality and return to wellness. A neighbour tells the story of how the previous owner of my home tried to poison a lovely gum tree guarding the property. In the stealth of the night, she took nutrients to feed its ailing body, sent love to its sorrowful heart and it survived.

I am taking supplements, have intravenous vitamin C and bioresonance therapy on a regular basis. Blood tests are carried out every three months as they are an important guide to progress and also an indicator of change. Where possible, I eat local organic food and have learnt not to stress when this is not possible but bless what I have as there are few restaurants serving wholesome food. Reiki and acupuncture treatments are important to my regime for maintaining health. Fresh vegetable juicing is a daily 'must' as it is the fastest way to flood the body with nutrients; to gently detox and to support the removal of toxic substances resulting from unaware living and medical interventions. My lifestyle is transforming into how I love to live. When I have an occasional red wine, I source a biodynamic, chemical and pesticide free variety.

Yoga is a way of life and during thirty-something years of teaching, I learnt that slow simple movements, awareness of the body and conscious breathing are keys to unlocking tension and tightness. I had the gift of being able to work with the students' potpourri of ailments and body conditions at the one time, always in small classes. That was my job and I now apply this same concept to my healing. No one modality suits all but modifying a teaching to what works in the moment can be beneficial. There are many branches to the yoga and I take a bit from here and a bit from there to incorporate into my healing programme. For instance, I greet the morning with simple stretches and gentle asanas (yoga postures) followed by a time to meditate and go within. Strain can offset good work and it is important to gradually introduce healthy lifestyle choices into daily living.

Part of my weekly routine is to massage myself from top to toe with organic oil (sesame or almond are excellent) and for approximately thirty minutes, I sit in the sun (as naked as possible) or lie on a yoga mat or bed swathed in towels. This is known as abhyanga, an ancient Ayurvedic full-body massage to assist with the healing and detoxification process. It is a time to play relaxing music and to enjoy the moment while the skin absorbs the qualities of the oil. I have found this to be an excellent health tool to calm the nervous system and to assist my skin to repair from the damaging effects of chemotherapy. I then languish in a warm bath to which I add Epsom salts or hop under the shower, visualising a waterfall washing away toxins and dead skin as well as mental and emotional debris. Being in the shower or bath is grounding and as a consequence, insightful ideas, thoughts and messages can pop into my head. An Epsom salts foot bath can be a gentle alternative to draw out toxicity.

Molley and Jack were like a second mum and dad to me when I was growing up. Molley's parents passed over when she was young and as a consequence, she lived on a relative's farm working for food and lodgings. Jack left England at the tender age of fifteen to carry his swag around the Australian countryside. They married in their forties and I was the fortunate youngster they loved and nurtured.

Their small backyard grew an abundance of vegetables and was a place where chickens freely roamed during the day and were locked safely away at night. Having no car, Molley and Jack walked everywhere, spent daily time in the garden touching the soil, drinking in the sun and being in nature. What I remember most is the gratitude they had for everything in their lives, nothing was taken for granted as they had experienced little nurturing, faded memories of family love and scarce material possessions. They were rarely ill and I remember wise words spoken but most of all, the advice, "When you're ill, rest." Their magic formula for recovery was to listen to the body and when it is lacking energy, know that its voice is saying, "It's time to rest." Today we tend to push the body and soldier on regardless. Molley and Jack's wisdom differed saying rest is how the body will heal and rejuvenate.

Listening to our body is a skill worth cultivating, especially when putting together a formula for healing disease that perhaps would not be a problem if this wisdom was taught at a young age. Did I not listen? For many years being a single mum with an ill daughter allowed little time to rest, however, I now hear the voices of those wonderful pioneers of my youth and I am listening.

Although we have been taught to believe we are victims of our genetic makeup the science of epigenetics says that it is environmental factors such as diet, chemicals and stress, together with mental and emotional factors that promote the expression of our genes. The work of Drs Wallach, Lan and Schrauzer (2014, p 504) has shown that many diseases thought to be genetically transmitted are in fact nutritional deficiencies that negatively impact the functions of DNA, RNA and enzymes. They say that eating a healthy diet and taking supplementation to provide the ninety essential nutrients can prevent and reverse most diseases.

The keys to good health include eating real food from nature's supermarket, protecting ourselves from excessive electromagnetic frequencies that have the ability to interfere with gene talk, exercising without strain, inhaling fresh air, soaking in the healing rays of the sun, connecting with the cycles of nature, resting and giving gratitude.

CHAPTER 13

I Love You Nan

I love staring into a candle's soft gentle light, watching it beckon, flicker and elongate. There is a meditation in yoga, watching the dancing flame, called Trataka and it is said the fire's essence cleanses the mind and calms its chaotic wobble. Candle light calls in the spirit for it loves to rest in that soft warm glow, however, the opposite can be said for the harsh electric lighting we live under night and day. Many blessings have been given to us from this technology but it has drastically changed our way of life.

Before the pull of a cord or the touch of a switch to flood a room with light, similar to rubbing a magic lamp for the genie to appear, we lived close to nature and flowed with the cycles of night and day. When the sun's rays kissed the dawn, we rose and when it sunk into the west, we slept. This enabled our bodies to heal and rejuvenate for darkness signals specific hormones to do what they do best, to release the flow of substances throughout our bodies to bring a return to balance.

The setting of the sun is a sacred time, to be still and let go of the day's wear and tear, to eat a small wholesome meal rather than the large evening feast we consume in the Western world, for the body is preparing to sleep and does not need a great deal of sustenance. Nature is closing its eyes and spirit, the silent witness, graciously departs allowing a time for rest and repair. Tomorrow is another day and a new adventure awaits. However, what happens when this cycle is disrupted and the physical body is not properly rested but forced to continue into the night? Our strong bodies gradually weaken and become susceptible to illness and a struggle to survive the day is now the name of the game. When this happens with regularity, sleep can no longer weave the magic of its healing touch to bring closure to the day. The holistic diamond of healing becomes tarnished, fractured and lifeless.

Perhaps cancer is a voice saying it does not have to be this way. When listening to the wisdom of our inner voice and making peace with the cancer, we embark on a journey of finding answers. It has been said that healing happens when we love every bit of ourselves. When we are not at war with our own bodies by waving the white flag instead of threatening with weapons of mass destruction, we are able to seek answers, make changes and above all, do what we are here to do, experience, learn, laugh and love. All easy to say, however!

Twelve months to the day I had completed my second chemotherapy treatment, I travelled the same journey to visit with Marie, Aron and the children. Instead of watching the slow dripping of chemicals into my veins, Aron met me at the railway station. It was Lily's birthday and I have finally accepted that the tug-of-war years between her demons and myself are done. My beautiful daughter is a wonderful teacher and my psychic friend, Mina, says Lily comes in the form of her higher being to sing to me when I am sleeping. This calms my soul.

Acceptance is the answer.

"It is what it is," says Aron and I have finally stopped struggling to change what is not mine to change.

I give gratitude for my life just as it is having learnt that life is a constant movement of what we call the ups and the downs. Sand in the hour glass is dwindling, my remaining time in this incarnation is short and every moment matters. However, I now know that the only thing I can control is how I respond to the unfolding of events in my life, to those I love and to the people of the Earth. For the silence of tomorrow is a place in the heart. When the door opens, I will walk through knowing I lived, loved, cried, laughed, touched the earth, felt the raindrops on my skin, the sun caressing my hair and heard the wind whispering secrets in my ear. However, there are still children and grandchildren to hug, sunsets to see, moments to share with friends, tears to cry and wrinkles to appear.

My hair is now short and white. My hairdresser cut every strand of chemo-laden hair from my head. "It's all gone," he had declared and that, I believe, is a milestone and perhaps the ending of a chapter in my book of life. Yes, I am in recovery from the treatment and there are ongoing doctor visits, blood tests to be taken and decisions to be made on whether to have further tests. I made it through the diagnosis, the chemotherapy, the operation and each day I am growing stronger in every facet of my being.

I like to reflect on the yogic analogy of the body being my carriage and know that it is becoming a beautifully restored vintage model with the horses pulling it, becoming more sensitive to the commands of the silent witness. When those bats of fear flap their wings and terror's cry is heard, I have a safe haven and I suspect that the cobbled road will blend into a smooth way. Dust will fly, stones will make dents in the side of the carriage and the horses trot will slow. However, this is just one of many journeys for the silent witness has travelled highways, sailed seas and not even the experience of cancer can touch it. It is the eternal adventurer, the captain of my ship, master of my soul.

Later that weekend when walking with my granddaughters, Jane said, "Nanny, can we do some meditation?"

As it was long ago that I had shown her a little yoga, I asked, "You didn't forget?"

"Of course, not," she replied flopping on the grass to sit cross-legged with hands resting on her knees, her soft brown eyes closing.

Three young girls on the brink of womanhood sat in the park with me, sharing a precious moment in time and a little of my teachings was passed on. That weekend, I was given many gifts of love. Cleveland, Deb and the twins arrived, the children wrote and produced a play and asked, "Can we do anything for you?" There were times I needed to rest but listening to the laughter and togetherness brought peace to my heart.

That night, ten-year-old Bray said, "I'll tuck you into bed Nanny." He pulled up the bed clothes, gave me a hug, said, "I love you Nan," and softly closed the door.

PART TWO

The Cure to Cancer is Prevention

*"Traditional physicians regard disease as a
failure of preventative health care, not as an
opportunity to test new drugs on patients."*

(Daniel Reid, 1993)

*This section contains information on what I consider to be contributory factors
towards today's cancer epidemic, information on natural medicine and lifestyle
changes that can assist to find that holistic diamond of wellness. It is for educational
purposes only and not medical advice. Cancer is serious and it is vital to consult
qualified practitioners.*

CHAPTER 14

Advanced Health Directive

*"You have the power to say,
'This is not how my story will end.'"*

(Unknown)

It is the legal right of every competent adult to say whether or not they wish to have recommended health care. While this may be somewhat easy when you can speak for yourself, it may not be the case if you are unconscious or unable to communicate your wishes and at a time when critical decisions need to be made. By completing an Advanced Health Directive, you can ensure your requests are known in the event of this happening.

I believe it is important for people of all ages to make an Advanced Health Directive. Accidents can happen and you may find yourself in an emergency ward where whatever Western medicine has to offer will be given. In some cases, it is the doctor or nurse who hears the patient's final words. If the wish of the person was for comfort only when the dying process begins, perhaps those last precious moments could be spent with loved ones.

The week leading up to Poppy's passing was spent in a hospital. Because of the way of Western medicine, he was treated until his last breath had been given, not as a gift but a tug-of-war between hospital staff and his soul's wish for completion. He endured an operation and was resuscitated on many occasions causing distress and pain to all levels of his being. I was spared the agony of watching this horrific process because I had endured a miscarriage and was prescribed bed rest. I had no input into what eventuated at this time and looking back doubt whether I had the knowledge or wisdom to consider another possibility. Today, if I had that opportunity, it would be a different story. Participating in a dignified passing is perhaps the final act of love, laying foundations for meaningful grief and future healing. I did not say my goodbyes and the grieving process remained unresolved for many years.

Treating terminal patients with little or no quality of life can prolong suffering that can be repeated again and again to deal with the crises as they arise. However, it does not have to be this way, another death can be chosen and when making an Advanced Health Directive, another choice can be whatever you request. For example, all treatment except mechanical life support and surgery or comfort only measures where medications are given to ease the pain and you are kept clean and warm. There are other options and we can choose them in advance.

Having the foresight to ensure that your wishes regarding treatment are known can save those you love from making decisions they may carry for the rest of their lives as guilt or unresolved grief. Relationships between family members can be fractured when wishes and beliefs differ. Your last words can be said to a loved one and not a stranger. It is important to discuss death and dying, medical procedures and your funeral prior to the time of passing. I consider my dying to be a sacred rite of passage, a celebration of my life. I believe my birth was farewelled from a place of love and my wish is to leave this life with a similar parting.

This chapter was inspired by an article written by Koren Helbig and published in the Courier Mail on 11 October, 2010. It brought back memories of the agony of Poppy's last week on Earth, an experience highlighting our cultural ignorance regarding the rite of passage we call death. I believe it is time we found a more humane and loving way to honour our last moments, those last tears and our final breath taking.

CHAPTER 15

Natural Medicine

*"Don't let your vision of the future be clouded
by those who have none."*

(Dr Ruth Cilento, 1993)

I envisage a world where cancer clinics modelled on today's best are available to everyone seeking wellness after a cancer diagnosis. Where integrative medicine is practised by doctors and researched by scientists working for the good of humanity and the planet. Even though it may not be possible to visit such a clinic, the information gleaned from a cyber exploration of the different methods of healing can add to knowledge when putting together a vision boat, finding the crew and deciding on treatments. For instance, watching *The Truth About Cancer* documentary or reading a book such as *Healing The Gerson Way* to incorporate therapies into a wellness plan to suit your lifestyle and resources.

Natural therapies are little discussed or known in Western oncology facilities. It is wise to do your own research, but seek practitioners to support and give guidance from a place of knowledge. Cancer is serious and so must we be in order to find the right formula to bring about our healing. It may seem overwhelming at first, but with time, research and listening to our inner guidance not the voice of fear, we can expect a miracle.

Below is a brief outline of some natural cancer treatments. The choices are varied and many but it is up to you to do your own research as every person is different and so is every cancer.

Artemisinin (Wormwood)

Artemisinin is an active ingredient isolated from the sweet wormwood plant called Artemisia annua of which there are approximately one-hundred-and-eighty known species, well-known ones being mugwort and tarragon. Its use as a treatment for malaria and parasite infections is documented in Chinese medical books dating back to approximately 340 AD. Artemisinin's effectiveness as an anti-malarial remedy was said to be rediscovered in the 1970's when a 'secret recipe', giving formulae and use, was found on a stone tablet in a tomb dating back to the Han Dynasty.

More recent studies, carried out by bioengineering professors at the University of Washington, concluded that artemisinin compounds could be developed into powerful anticancer drugs. This was thought to be the case because artemisinin reacts with iron to form free radicals that kill cells. Since cancer cells are high in iron, they are susceptible to the toxic effect of artemisinin (Lai, Sasaki and Singh, 2005). Artemisinin has been used for thousands of years but modern science is showing promise that this could be refined into an effective and safe cancer killer. Artemisinin supplements are available from the Allergy Research Group - website: www.iherb.com/c/allergy-research-group. It is important to seek the advice of an integrative practitioner with training in natural medicine as to suitability and dosage.

This plant is named after Artemis the moon goddess and twin sister to Apollo, the sun god. She is portrayed as a wild virgin huntress, mistress of untamed beasts, the protector of pregnancy, childbirth and the sisterhood; a powerful image for a breast cancer treatment.

Dendritic Cell Therapy

Dendritic cells play an important part in detecting viruses, fungi, bacteria and malignant cells as well as assisting the immune system to deal with disease. In dendritic cell therapy, it is these cells taken from the patient's own blood that are used to make a vaccine to support the body to fight cancer.

In 2010 in the United States of America, dendritic vaccination for metastatic prostate cancer was approved as an effective treatment. The Nobel Prize in Physiology and Medicine was awarded in 2011 to the researchers who discovered the role dendritic cells play in tackling cancer cells.

Research is being carried out to study dendritic cell therapy which could emerge as a non-toxic vaccination for treating certain types of cancer. Dendritic vaccines have for many years, played a crucial role in integrative immunotherapy programmes such as the Gorter Model. This is an integrative approach incorporating hyperthermia and immune restoration using mistletoe, nutrient infusions, ozone, cannabis and lifestyle changes according to the patient's needs. For further information see website: www.robert-gorter.info.medical-center-cologne.com.

Essiac Tea

Here is another colourful tale beginning the day a woman was given an herbal blend by an Ojibway Indian shaman who said it would cure her breast cancer. Some thirty years later a Canadian nurse, Rene Caisse, was told the story by the same woman and Essiac tea (Caisse spelt backwards) came into being. Following the successful healing of a relative using the formulae, Rene Caisse opened a clinic which operated for approximately eight years. The success of this clinic in claiming to have treated between three to six hundred people per week, attracted the notice of the medical authorities and so began a saga of harassment and persecution that lasted for over fifty years. During this time, Nurse Caisse was offered one million dollars for the formula which she refused as there were no guarantees patients would be treated free of charge.

It is the belief of the Ojibway and indeed indigenous peoples from all over the world that it is the plant's spirit essence that truly heals and it is said a blend of herbs can enhance healing. An example is Essiac tea containing herbs such as burdock root, sheep sorrel, turkey rhubarb root and slippery elm bark, all of which have immune-boosting properties and protect against free radical damage. However, we need to remember the method used to prepare the formula, correct dosage, ratio of ingredients as well as the quality of the herbs used are important to success. Essiac Tea can boast a long history of success in assisting cancer patients to maintain health. A modern-day recipe named *Flor Essence*, based on the original formula but containing additional herbs such as watercress, blessed thistle, red clover and kelp is available from: www. florahealth.com.

FLAXSEED OIL AND COTTAGE CHEESE

The flaxseed oil and cottage cheese diet is the work of German biochemist and physicist, Dr Johanna Budwig (1908-2003) who was nominated to receive a Noble Prize seven times. Finding seriously ill patients, including cancer patients, to be deficient in essential fatty acids she put together a recipe to correct this imbalance. This consisted of organic cottage cheese or quark, a source of sulphur-based protein, and flaxseed oil, rich in Omega-3. Dr Budwig believed that a deficiency in today's Western diet of healthy fats is a major contributing factor to escalating health problems. She also believed that this has come about by changing the nature of natural oils in order to transport large quantities to supermarkets and for long shelf life. All margarines, hydrogenated and partially hydrogenated fats and oils as well as many processed poly-unsaturated fats include these chemically altered harmful oils that obstruct the oxidation process within the body, contributing to ill health. Daniel Reid (1993, p 384) explains, "These artificial fats oxidise immediately upon exposure to air, the moment you unseal the can or the bottle, and they continue to oxidise inside your system, setting up a chain reaction of molecular mayhem that destroys cells and disrupts vital functions much faster than your body's natural capacity to defend itself from such damage." Healthy fats to consume for optimal health consist of organic butter from grass fed animals, cold-pressed, organic coconut and olive oil, avocados and nut butters.

Believing what we take into the body must be as nature intended, Dr

Budwig's protocol included a special dietary programme. She reported documented cases of not only cancer recovery but also benefits in healing diabetes, eczema, psoriasis, arthritis and hormone and neurological imbalances.

Today, the Budwig Center situated in Malaga, Spain, offers the Budwig diet together with supportive therapies such as hyperthermia, Vega testing, bio-energetic restoration, reflexology, parbiomagnetism therapy, infrared sauna, psychotherapy, dietary and lifestyle support. Dr Budwig's dietary information, recipes and articles can be downloaded from website: www.budwigcenter.com.

Hyperthermia

In 1868, Dr Peter Busch discovered that fever can kill cancer cells leaving healthy cells intact, however, he was not the first to make this observation as physicians have used this knowledge for thousands of years. It is told that it was Parmenides (born approx. 515 BC), Greek physician and philosopher who said, "I would cure all diseases if I only could produce fever." Fever is the body's natural way to activate the immune system to fight disease and today, integrative cancer clinics use sophisticated state of the art technology to take the body to high temperatures. This is known as hyperthermia. Treatment can involve the whole body or be localised such as in breast cancer hyperthermia where microwave energy is directed to the tumour. When used as a complementary therapy, side effects from chemotherapy can be reduced and the effectiveness of treatments such as intravenous vitamin C and laetrile is enhanced.

The Medical Center Cologne (MCC), Germany, say, "Research has made it clear that fever is not the enemy; it is the friend of healing. This scientific rationale, supported by thousands of research studies, provides the basis for hyperthermia treatment at the Medical Center Cologne and other medical centers in Europe, Japan, and worldwide." Interesting research on their website says that a fever in childhood or adulthood may protect against the later onset of malignant disease. Researchers are finding that suppressing childhood infections and fever through vaccines and medications can increase vulnerability to cancer in later life. Frequent use of medications or antibiotics to arrest a fever impairs the immune system by suppressing the trigger (fever) that activates the immune response. For further information visit website: www.gorter-model.org/hyperthermia.

Insulin Potentiated Therapy (IPT)

Insulin potentiated therapy involves an injection of insulin to entice the cancer cell membrane to become open to receiving the sugar it craves and thrives on. An intravenous glucose solution is then administered that may contain substances such as vitamin C or selenium to weaken and destroy tumour cells. This method is also used to deliver low dose chemotherapy enabling the poison to go directly into the cancer cells with less damage to healthy cells. Hair loss, organ damage and changes to the DNA experienced with the standard chemotherapy treatments can be averted.

I am wondering why this method is not widely used along with blood testing to determine which chemotherapy agents are likely to work and to determine the level of circulating tumour cells (CTC) in the body (see: Part Four - Genostics Testing). Why are we not using successful complementary treatments to accomplish what chemotherapy alone cannot? Therapies to alleviate circulating tumour cells that are responsible for metastasis and being slower to reproduce are not destroyed by chemotherapy or radiotherapy.

Intravenous Vitamin C

As a deficiency is often found in cancer patients, this method can infuse a high dose of vitamin C into the blood stream to increase intake. It can boost the immune system, strengthen collagen to assist in preventing cancer from spreading, stimulate the growth of cancer fighting cells, neutralise free radicals and improve energy levels. Toxicity from radiation and chemotherapy treatments can be lessened, the response to these therapies improved and the body's natural healing systems given a boost.

The Riordan Clinical Research Institute (RCRI) have clinically tested and researched the potential of intravenous vitamin C therapy for over thirty years. They found an improvement in the patient's quality of life, a reduction in inflammation and vitamin C to be a toxic cancer cell killer at high doses without harming healthy cells (www.riordanclinic.org/research-study-ivc-protocol).

An interesting study showing the effectiveness of intravenous vitamin C was conducted by Dr Atsuo Yanagisawa from the Japanese College of Intravenous Therapy. He administered large doses as a pre-treatment to half the men entering the Fukushima Nuclear Power Plant following the 2011 earthquake and tsunami. After completing the risky work, careful medical evaluations showed them to be clear of DNA damage and precancerous indicators that would otherwise have resulted from the radiation. The untreated workers presented with DNA damage and precancerous indicators but were then given similar post-treatment for a couple of months and completely recovered.

Dr Yanagisawa has published books on cardiology, chelation therapy, nutrition, coaching and vitamin C for cancer. In 2011, he was inducted into the Orthomolecular Medicine Hall of Fame for his pioneering contribution to intravenous therapy in Japan.

LAETRILE

Nitrilosides are natural compounds found in many foods such as lima beans, clover, sorghum and are derived from the kernel of various fruits, including apricot and peach pits, apple seeds, quince seeds and the berry family, especially those growing wild. One of the most common nitriloside being amygdalin. Scientists have observed the extremely low cancer incidence in people living on a primitive diet high in nitriloside-rich foods. These include the Hunza people from the Himalayas who grow apricot trees and eat the fruit either fresh or dried, all year round. Their diet consists mainly of fresh vegetables, fruit and grain such as millet and buckwheat, supported by drinking living water and leading a lifestyle where toxins are kept to a minimum. The Hopi and Navajo Indians who live to a healthy old age, cancer free, eat a traditional diet including foods rich in amygdalin such as cassava. The Eskimos living their traditional way, eating food such as the meat from the caribou (who eat grasses high in nitrilosides) and the Australian aboriginal people are other examples. When these people change to a Western diet, statistics show that degenerative diseases increase.

The use of apricot pits and bitter almond oil for healing can be dated back to ancient Egyptian and Chinese medicine. Medieval Eastern Mediterranean literature describes bitter almond containing amygdalin as not only an important food but as having medicinal value for treating many ailments. The physician Assaf Harofeh who authored the *Book of Asaph*, (thought to be one of the oldest written medical texts in the world) said that almond oil fortifies the heart, relieves stress, and heals the intestines. The oil of bitter almonds was found to be beneficial in treating many illnesses such as headaches, general pains, cough, breathing problems, lungs, kidney stones, liver ailments, renal obstructions, impotence and menstruation, (Lev and Amar, 2008, p 92).

Modern-day research has found nitrilosides to be important to health and to play a part in the cancer prevention story. One such researcher was Dr Ernst Krebs Jr (1911-1996) who perfected a patented formula proposed by his father, Dr Ernst Krebs (1877-1970). Known as Laetrile (sometimes called vitamin B17), this was successfully used to treat cancer by renowned doctors such as Dr Shigeaki Sakai in Japan and Dr Ernesto Contreras, founder of the Oasis of Hope Hospital, Tiguana, Mexico where it is still used today. Dr Alfred Nieper (1928-1998), one of the world's most respected cancer specialists, during a visit to the United States in 1972 told news reporters: "After more than twenty years of such specialised work, I have found non-toxic nitrilosides - that is, Laetrile - far superior to any other known cancer treatment or preventative. In my opinion, it is the only existing possibility for the ultimate control of cancer" (Griffin, 1997, p 106).

Laetrile is not legally approved for use in Australia or the United States of America. Why are toxic drugs such as chemotherapy that have a small success rate approved and therapies shown to be effective and safe demonised? The answer in part is that the high cost of conducting trials does not make a non-toxic plant that cannot be patented profitable.

MISTLETOE (VISUM ALBUM)

Mistletoe, considered by the Druids to be sacred, was believed to be an antidote to all poisons and used in the treatment of infertility. Scientist, philosopher and the founder of anthroposophical medicine, Rudolf Steiner (1861-1925) brought mistletoe into the realm of modern science in 1920 as a possible cancer treatment. It was his colleague, Dr Ita Wegman (1876-1943) who developed a formula called Iscar which later became known as Iscador. Dr Wegman was instrumental in founding a non-profit organisation, The Society for Cancer Research. Today, this consists of the Lukas Clinic in Germany and the Hiscia Institute located in Switzerland, where Iscador is produced and research conducted. Recent cancer medicines made from mistletoe are marketed as Abnoba, Helixor, Eurixor and Lektinol.

Mistletoe is a semi-parasitic, bushy plant that grows on deciduous and coniferous trees such as oak, apple, birch, willow, poplar, elm, pine and spruce. The type of tumour and constitution of the patient determine which host tree is chosen for therapy. As the plant's healing abilities change with the seasons, twice a year harvesting is important to its therapeutic value. In summer, viscotoxins known to support the breaking down of tumours by dissolving the walls of cancer cells are produced. In winter, the plant yields lectins which inhibit the growth of cancer cells and stimulate immunity.

Mistletoe is widely used by medical doctors in Europe as a complementary treatment to conventional therapies. As it is adversely affected by the digestive juices, it is usually given by injection under the skin, always by a qualified practitioner. It has been shown to reduce the side effects from treatments such as chemotherapy, surgery and radiotherapy, to improve quality of life and to be an immune stimulant.

ORGANIC COFFEE ENEMAS

Many civilisations have recorded the use and benefits of enemas for inner cleansing, examples being ancient Egyptian medical texts written on papyrus and Patanjali's famous work unifying yoga, known as the

Yoga Sutras. It is said that Hippocrates prescribed water enemas some 2,500 years-ago.

It is told that the effectiveness of coffee enemas was discovered by accident towards the end of World War I in Germany when medications were non-existent. In an attempt to help the thousands of injured soldiers suffering terrible pain, a nurse was said to use coffee as it was the only sterile solution available. It worked. The remedy, widely used from then on as a therapeutically administered organic coffee enema, was shown to bring quick relief from pain, reduce inflammation and to support in detoxifying the liver and the gallbladder. This therapy could be found in the Merck Manual of Medical Information until the early nineteen seventies. Today, integrative oncology clinics successfully use coffee enemas to assist with detoxification such as moving toxic dead cancer cells from the body.

Information on coffee enemas and how to take them can be found in Charlotte Gerson and Morton Walker's book called *The Gerson Therapy*. The Gerson website has a store where enema kits can be purchased.

OZONE THERAPY

Yoga teaches that by increasing oxygen intake through deep breathing, gentle exercise and intention, the blood flow can be purified by eliminating harmful toxins. It has been shown that saturating the body with oxygen enables a decrease in respiration and heartbeat, thereby improving health and increasing the lifespan. Every cell in our body dances in merriment when partnered by molecules of oxygen. However, this is not the case with cancer cells that thrive and grow in a low oxygen environment, a fact discovered by the 1931 Nobel Prize winner for Physiology and Medicine, Dr Otto Warburg (1883-1970).

By taking the time to consciously deep breathe, visit, or live in, natural environments and by having an awareness of breathing patterns, the flow of oxygen is increased throughout the body. When feeling angry, sad or fearful the breath is impeded, however, by relaxing and breathing into the part of the body where the emotion is felt, we can restore balance.

Imagine those molecules of oxygen carrying brooms and sweeping away toxic emotions just as they do toxic debris.

Modern medicine uses a method known as ozone therapy which is oxygen with an extra molecule (03). It works by flooding the blood stream with oxygen to selectively kill cancer cells while being non-toxic to healthy cells. Ozone has bacterial, fungicidal and virucidal properties, used for a wide range of degenerative diseases such as cancer, cardiovascular, diabetes, liver and kidney. It is an effective complementary treatment known to soften the aftermath of chemotherapy. Modern research is taking a close look at oxygen therapy in regard to heart disease, AIDS and dentistry.

Ozone therapy is used without legal restrictions in countries such as Germany, Russia and Cuba and included in treatment programmes at some of the Mexican cancer clinics. The well-known, Ozone Research Center, Havana, Cuba, offers medical ozone treatment and research facilities as well as being involved in the use of ozone for sanitation, waste water treatment, and the design, construction and installation of ozone generators. Ozone treated swimming pools are common in Europe, eliminating the problems associated with chlorine toxicity.

Ozone can be administered in a number of ways. For example, by autohemotherapy which is a technique used to withdraw a small amount of blood from the vein. Ozone or a homeopathic agent can be added and then the same blood is injected back into a muscle or vein to encourage the immune system to tackle debris found in the blood as a result of illness. Other methods include rectal ozone insufflations, a process similar to receiving an enema and by external application such as ozonated oil used to treat skin problems and fungal infections. This is an effective way to support breast healing following surgery.

CHAPTER 16

Alternative and Integrative Clinics

"The key to any successful therapy is education.
Find out what's available and determine
what you can believe in and support.
The greatest thing you can do for yourself is self-
education, rather than thinking that mainstream
treatment is all you have and all that there is.
That's just not true."

Dr David Walker, founder of the
Medical Arts Center, Mexico
(Fortson 2011, p 137)

I love the colourful stories of those courageous doctors and scientists who despite persecution from the cancer industry continue their work hoping the seeds they are planting will blossom in a future time. Perhaps that time is now with more people coming into awareness of the suppression of safe and effective cancer therapies. The cancer situation as we know it today would change if the knowledge kept in indigenous circles, suppressed discoveries by renowned scientists and clinically proven natural therapies were pooled for research and trial.

Many centres are having remarkable success with treating cancer and degenerative disease. For instance, the suppression of successful non-toxic treatments for cancer in the United States of America has led to the establishment of the Mexican clinics. These are reputed to be some of the world's best, boasting a combination of the finest doctors and cutting-edge treatments. Frank Cousineau and Andrew Schonberg have offered information on the best of the Mexican clinics in their book, *Cancer Defeated: How Rich and Poor Alike Get Well in Foreign Clinics.*

Some well-known clinics are:

TIJUANA HOXSEY CLINIC

"Do not go where the path may lead, go instead where there is no path and leave a trail" (Ralph Waldo Emerson, 1803-1882).

The tale handed down through the generations on the birthing of the famous Hoxsey herbal formulae began in 1840 when John Hoxsey found a malignant tumour on the right hock of his prize stallion. After putting the animal to pasture and subsequently witnessing the healing that followed, he experimented with the herbs he had seen the animal eating that were not part of its normal diet. This resulted in an herbal topical salve, a powder and an internal tonic that were successfully used to treat animals with cancer. These formulas were passed down through the generations and were first tried on people by his grandson, John Hoxsey, a veterinarian. His son, Harry Hoxsey, opened the first Hoxsey Cancer Clinic in Texas in 1924 that became the world's largest privately-owned cancer clinic with branches in seventeen states. The clinic's success triggered a thirty-five-year war with the medical authorities. Despite thousands of patients testifying they had been healed and the paste being medically found to cure external cancer, he was blocked from carrying out scientific evaluations.

In 1963, Harry Hoxsey's chief nurse, Mildred Nelson, took the treatment to Tijuana and established the Bio-Medical Center as it is now known and continues to claim high success rates. Mildred Nelson died in 1999 after appointing her sister as chief administrator and today, this clinic is equipped with the latest diagnostic equipment. Therapies include herbal medicine, vitamin and mineral supplements, diet and lifestyle counselling and conventional medical treatments when necessary. The clinic says the Hoxsey legacy of healing lives on. It is interesting to note that like Rene Caisse, Harry Hoxsey was said to have refused a large sum of money for his formulae due to the fact that treatment for those who could not afford to pay was not guaranteed. Information on the Hoxsey clinic can be found at website: www.hoxseybiomedical.com.

Burzynski Clinic

Mike Adams (2017) said, *"You cannot kill an idea with violence. You cannot kill the truth with threats. The light of truth always wins."*

The year 1967 marked the beginning of this story when Dr Stanislaw Burzynski, a physician and biochemist-researcher, identified naturally occurring peptides in the human body that can control cancer growth. He called these antineoplastons. Finding a noticeable deficiency of these in cancer patients, he developed the use of these biologically active peptides in diagnosing, preventing and treating cancer. It is a non-toxic approach with long-term recovery for many cancer patients, particularly effective for those suffering lymphomas and brain cancers.

Not long before my cancer journey began, I watched *Burzynski the Movie* telling the tale of an ongoing battle with the medical establishment over a cancer treatment based on the body's natural defense system to combat the disease. There are many doctors successfully treating cancer with non-toxic therapies that differ from toxic mainstream treatments offering little success. This low success rate has been shown in a study giving the overall contribution of curative and adjuvant cytotoxic chemotherapy to a five-year survival in adults as an estimated 2.3% in Australia and 2.1% in the United States of America. It was stated in the conclusion that it is clear cytotoxic chemotherapy only makes a minor contribution to cancer survival and to justify the enormous funding and the impact on quality of life, further evaluation is urgently required (Morgan, Ward and Barton, 2004).

Situated in Texas and established in 1977, the Burszynski clinic is one of many offering a successful non-toxic approach. For further information see website: www.burzynskiclinic.com.

GERSON INSTITUTE

Dr Max Gerson (2002) said, *"Our soil must be normal, no artificial fertilisers should be used, no poisons, no sprays which go into the soil and poison it. Whatever grows on a poisoned soil carries poison, too, and that is our food, our fruit and vegetables. I am convinced that the soil is our external metabolism. It is not really far removed from our bodies. We depend on it."*

The Gerson Institute is a non-profit organisation located in San Diego, California, established in 1977 by Charlotte Gerson the youngest daughter of Dr Max Gerson, founder of the therapy in the 1930's. The Institute offers education and training in a nutrition-based, non-toxic treatment for patients suffering chronic degenerative diseases and searching for a return to health through holistic healing. Based on the belief that cancer is a result of toxicity and a vitamin and mineral deficiency, the programme is about detoxing the body and rebuilding the immune system with nutrients by flooding it with organic vegetarian food. Being one of the best-known nutrition-based protocols, aspects of the Gerson therapy are used as a foundation for treatment by many practitioners. The two registered clinics offering treatment are: the Gerson Clinic in Mexico and the Gerson Health Centre in Hungary.

Charlotte Gerson believes when the immune system is fully operational it does not heal selectively, when enzymes, minerals and other nutrients are restored to the body, everything heals. Patients present with many diseases and carry on to fully restore the body's defense system and defeat their disease. Ms Gerson tells us that when you truly heal, the whole body heals. The Gerson website offering a wealth of information can be found at: www.gerson.org.

It is Andrew Saul's belief: "If the Gerson therapy was permitted inside the United States, and I believe it should be, we would see a dramatic decrease in death from cancer. I estimate it would go down by fifty percent, or possibly more so" (Mazzucco, 2010).

HOPE4CANCER CLINIC

Dr Tony Jimenez (2015) pointed to his head and said, *"A negative thought can kill you faster than a bad germ."*

Situated in Baja, Mexico, Hope4Cancer says cancer stem cells do not show up on regular diagnostic equipment, are not destroyed by treatments such as chemotherapy and radiation and can in time, morph into a more aggressive cancer. These issues can be addressed by treatments tailored to each individual's needs and can include ozone, hyperthermia, enzyme, laetrile, intravenous vitamin C, nutrition and immune enhancing and detoxification therapies. Therapies such as Sono-Photo Dynamic Therapy (SPDT), combining light and sound technology to destroy cancer cells in a non-invasive, non-toxic procedure and Rigvir cancer virotherapy are options. Discovered by Professor Aina Muceniece in the 1960's, Rigvir virotherapy is approved in Latvia for the treatment of melanoma. It is non-toxic, selectively targeting cancer cells, leaving healthy cells untouched with clinical success in treating cancers such as stomach, prostate, pancreatic, lung, kidney and uterine. Training and certification for physicians is offered at the International Virotherapy Center (IVC), Latvia.

Medical director and oncologist, Dr Tony Jimenez's recipe for stopping cancer cells that are triggered in our bodies all the time is to maintain a strong immune system, adhere to a strict nutritional regimen, remove toxins and microbial influences, oxygenate, hydrate, exercise and keep a strong emotional and spiritual balance. For further information see website: www.hope4cancer.com.

OASIS OF HOPE

Dr Francisco Contreras (2013) said, *"There's always something that can be done, even if it's only to hold the patient's hand and pray."*

The Oasis of Hope Hospital is a renowned institution for the treatment of cancer using alternative and conventional methods based on recent research. It was founded in 1963 by the late Dr Ernesto Contreras, an advocate of body, mind and spirit medicine and a pioneer of integrative oncology. Treatments used include high-dose intravenous vitamin C, ozone, laetrile, stem cell therapy, nutraceuticals, low dose chemotherapy and radiation. Genetic testing is carried out to determine chemotherapy and natural medicine suitability for each patient. It is the belief here that there is nearly always an emotional component to cancer and therefore the psychological and spiritual needs of the patient are considered to be as important as the physical. The website can be found at: www.oasisofhope.com.

Oncologist and surgeon, Dr Francisco Contreras is the director, president and chairman of the Oasis of Hope. When speaking on the 2013 online Cure to Cancer Summit, he commented that there is a lot of proven and published work to say integrative therapies are more effective than conventional methods. He stressed the importance of preparing the body for chemotherapy with supplementary treatment to lessen dosage, deal with side effects and enhance the overall result. He said follow-up therapy is most important as the history of cancer is that it comes back with a vengeance and a lifestyle change to support the immune system can ensure a quality life even when living with cancer.

Dr Contreras has authored many books including, *Hope, Medicine & Healing, 50 Critical Cancer Answers, The Hope of Living Cancer Free, The Coming Cancer Cure, Beating Cancer and Dismantling Cancer*.

Sanoviv Medical Institute

This Institute says: *"Sanoviv can assist you in understanding cancer from a different perspective; one of hope, care and respect, a perspective that includes options that make sense, and one that includes you as a full partner in your healing. Despite the fact that cancer is a serious disease, it can be overcome."*

Sanoviv is located in Rosarito, Mexico and was founded by Dr Myron Wentz, a microbiologist and immunologist who studied for forty years to discover what creates healthy cells. It is a hospital and research centre model for future health care, built from non-toxic building materials, free from electromagnetic frequencies, offering a beautiful relaxing environment complete with organic meals.

Sanoviv says conventional approaches such as chemotherapy and radiation cannot be used continually because the high toxicity and side effects are often more dangerous to a long life than the cancer itself. Taking body chemistry and personal history into consideration, treatments are put together using cutting-edge diagnostic equipment and evidence-based traditional and natural therapies. These include dendritic cell therapy, hyperthermia, rife therapy, intravenous sodium bicarbonate, psychology, nutrition, dentistry, chiropractic, diet and lifestyle counselling. Sanoviv's goal is to understand the uniqueness of each person's disease, saying cancer is a group of more than one hundred distinct and different illnesses that begin with cellular abnormalities. The genetic, lifestyle, and environmental components that may have contributed to its occurrence are taken into consideration. Further information can be found at website: www.sanoviv.com.

PARACELSUS CLINIC

The Paracelsus Clinic says, *"Medicine is not only a science; it is also an art. It does not consist of compounding pills and plasters; it deals with the very processes of life, which must be understood before they may be guided."*

The Paracelsus Clinic, founded in 1958 and situated in a beautiful part of Switzerland, use what they term 'Biological Medicine' to get to the root cause of each person's illness and to support the body's healing abilities through natural remedies. It is world renowned, offering sophisticated integrative medical practices to detoxify, strengthen and build a healthy immune system, a cornerstone to healing and maintaining health. The latest diagnostic testing is used and when needed, conventional medicine in conjunction with other therapies to treat cancer, heart and digestive disorders, autoimmune and infectious diseases such as Lyme, to name but a few.

I was interested to learn that breast is the most common cancer seen at the Clinic due to woman either refusing conventional treatment or therapies post-surgery, because of the terrible after effects for a relatively small improvement in their prognosis. Paracelsus tells us that of the hundreds of patients with localised breast cancer seen over the years, not one has experienced metastasis and claims success, even in advanced cases. It is said the key here is in supporting an intensive shift of the internal environment that gave rise to the cancer in the first place.

It was Dr Rau, the medical director of the Clinic for over twenty-four years, who evolved biological medicine into the comprehensive healing system that has led to the centre becoming a leader for alternative medicine in Europe. He has published five books including *Biological Medicine* and *The Swiss Diet for Optimal Health*. The Paracelsus Wellness Clinic recently opened in Kuala Lumpur. Further information can be found at website: www.paracelsus.ch.

A special bond can quickly form when meeting another on a similar journey who has an understanding of the treatments you are having or the diet you follow. One such person is Kathy who travels long distances to pull together integrative therapies to support her healing and considers visits to the Paracelsus Clinic to be a vital part of her personal healing regime. She speaks of innovative therapies offered that are not available in her home country, Australia, nor sadly are they on the radar of most health professionals in this country.

German Cancer Clinics

The 3E Centre, Germany, says, "*Wise patients learn that tumors are only symptoms, and destroying or removing the tumor does not mean the cancer is gone. Patients need accurate information to help them not only get rid of the cancer, but to learn to regain optimum health and to adjust their diets and lifestyle to maintain that health.*"

It is eleven years since my friend, Anna, was diagnosed with breast cancer. With two young boys to guide into manhood and an estranged partner, major lifestyle changes could not be made at the time and stress continued to sabotage her every action. Two years later, Anna had a mastectomy and began the battle with brain and liver tumours which she won mainly due to two trips to a clinic in Germany. At the clinic, she was offered integrative medicine, the best conventional and complementary methods available, used with no legal restrictions. Anna's cancer journey is not over as metastatic cancer is now showing in her bones and finances do not allow for another trip to Germany. However, having learnt a lot about the effectiveness of integrative medicine, Anna is finding her own unique way through local resources.

Hyperthermia is one of the treatments Anna talks about and the German doctors have mastered this therapy, knowing that fever has a devastating effect on cancer cells while leaving healthy cells intact. Mistletoe, ozone, intravenous vitamin C, dendritic vaccines, magnetic field and nutritional therapies are some of the treatments offered at the clinics. Diagnostic tests that can indicate what chemotherapy and natural therapies will work best with each person's particular cancer are another option.

Anna says there are six clinics boasting a world-class reputation. She loved the Bed and Breakfast style accommodation and has fond memories of people from all over the world who shared her cancer journey for brief moments in time. Her eyes light when she tells such stories and tears glisten for those who passed but have left a legacy, the remembrance of just how bright the human spirit can shine.

The question is, "Why can Anna not receive the same ongoing treatment here in Australia and why did she have to travel to Germany in the first place?"

Andrew Scholberg's book, *German Cancer Breakthrough: Your Guide to Top German Clinics* offers information on some of the German clinics.

Dr Nicholas Gonzalez

Dr Kelly Brogan, holistic women's health psychiatrist and author of *A Mind of Your Own*, said, *"Dr Gonzalez was a clinical genius, an activist and a visionary who changed the course of medicine for all those willing to let go of the old paradigm."*

Dr Gonzalez was in practice in New York from 1987 to 2015. Over thirty years of research and clinical experience resulted in a unique nutritional approach to cancer and other degenerative diseases such as Lyme, allergies, autoimmune disorders and chronic fatigue. Treatments included personalised nutrition, supplements, large doses of pancreatic enzymes and detoxification, depending on the patient's metabolic type. The detoxification process incorporated daily coffee enemas to help the liver eliminate dead cancer cells broken down by the pancreatic enzymes.

I have included information on the late Dr Gonzalez's work as his records show lasting wellness for patients unmatched in the journals of allopathic medicine. Valuable information can be gained by listening to his video presentations or delving into his written work. His wife founded The Nicholas Gonzalez Foundation, a non-profit foundation for educating and training doctors in The Gonzalez Protocol. Information can be found on website: www.dr-gonzalez.com.

CHAPTER 17

Dentistry

"So, we took out those three root canals when
she had three to six months to live.
And, that was six years ago, and she
is still alive today, and MRI
cannot find the tumour any more. It went away."

(Hal Huggins, DDS)

Clinics and practitioners working with dentistry as part of the cancer therapy remove root canal and amalgam mercury fillings and generally free teeth of bacteria before commencing other therapies. The Paracelsus Clinic in Switzerland is an example of a renowned clinic using holistic dentistry including the removal of root canal fillings prior to commencing treatment. In 2004, on examining the records of one hundred and fifty women admitted to the clinic with breast cancer, it was found that one hundred and forty-seven had one or more root canal-filled teeth on the same meridian as the original breast cancer tumour. The connection between the teeth and specific organs and systems in the body through the energy meridians has been successfully mapped by ancient Eastern medicine. When a tooth contains a toxic substance such as amalgam, is infected or damaged, an imbalance of energy occurs in the body affecting the connecting organ and the overall health suffers.

Independent research scientist, Dr Hulga Clark (1993, p 81) believed that plastic fillings could be toxic and wrote, "My recent tests show that most varieties of dental plastics contain known tumorigens as did amalgams, of course. In fact, I believe that toxic dental materials we suck on day and night are largely responsible for our cancer epidemic and the abnormal T-cell ratio in AIDS." Carcinogens such as nickel, chromium and cobalt can be used in metal crowns. Composite fillings can contain toxic substances such as aluminium, strontium and formaldehyde which is known to cause skin, eye, nose and throat irritations and respiratory problems including asthma and fatigue. Dr Sherry Rogers' (2002, p 144) research revealed that the glues or adhesives used to cement fillings and crowns in teeth can produce a wide range of symptoms from triggering a heart attack or sudden death, to malignant tumours and much more. A biocompatibility test is now available to determine which dental materials will cause less sensitivity and immune system rejection.

Dr Weston Price (1870-1948), a founding member of the American Dental Association, was well known for his study of isolated communities and traditional diets while searching for an answer to today's dental and degenerating health issues. He concluded that modern denatured food resulting in nutritional deficiencies was the major cause of chronic illness and tooth decay. As far back as 1910, Dr Price discovered that many diseases can originate from root canals because of the highly toxic bacteria that can be kept alive within root canal teeth to make its way into the bloodstream. Circulatory, kidney and heart disease, arthritis, mental illness, pregnancy complications and cancer are some of the diseases that may result and can take decades to appear. More recent, the Toxic Element Research Foundation (TERF) after thirty years of research and using the most up-to-date DNA testing equipment, has brought to public awareness the potential problems associated with dental materials and procedures (www.terfinfo.com). Potent toxins and bad bacteria found in the teeth can weaken the immune system, cause acidity, upset the ratio of good and bad gut bacteria and block the energy systems throughout the body. Toxicity in teeth plays a part in the cancer story.

Dr Hal Huggins (1937-2014) was a leading pioneer in investigating and treating medical problems caused by toxic dental materials. He developed a protocol for lessening the risk of triggering the onset of autoimmune diseases that can be a problem when removing amalgams and root canal teeth. With a master's degree in immunology and over forty years of research and experience, Dr Huggins wrote many books on the dangers of present-day dentistry. In an article called, *DNA Studies Confirm Dr Western Price's Century-old Findings*, he wrote: "In order for the immune system to focus on healing, all other offending dental materials should be removed (mercury, copper, implants, tattoos and nickel crowns) so that the immune system can deal with the bacterial challenge instead of the bacteria plus toxic metals." Tattoos are bits of mercury that have lodged in the tissue or jaw during dental procedures.

A doctor or practitioner conversed in holistic cancer therapy should be able to recommend the appropriate time to have this work carried out. It is wise to look for a holistic or biological dentist who knows how to safely remove amalgam fillings so as not to risk mercury being released into your system. If this occurs, symptoms such as trembling, fatigue, depression, anxiety, insomnia, brain fog, numbness, tunnel vision, migrating pain or memory loss may present. Mercury poisoning is linked to health issues such as central nervous system disorders, autoimmune and cardiovascular disease, heart, kidney and liver damage, visionary impairment, ADD, fibromyalgia and cancer. It can cause the same type of damage to the brain found in Alzheimer's patients. Dr Boyd Haley, a researcher on the role mercury, dental amalgams, and thimerosal play in degenerative disease and now-retired professor and chair of the Department of Chemistry, University of Kentucky, wrote in a report to the FDA: "It seems very reasonable to consider a hypothesis that mercury would be the major contributor to early onset Alzheimer's disease."

Mercury is used in paints, light switches, thermometers, barometers, thermostats and contaminates the atmosphere by incineration of discarded products such as fluorescent lights, batteries, electrical appliances and from coal burning emissions. Mercury has been dumped into waterways contaminating the sea life thereby destroying a food source and income for local people. One famous instance is the story of Minamata, a fishing village in Japan. In the 1950's industrial waste containing methylmercury spilled into Minamata Bay resulting in deformities, debilitation and death. As methylmercury transfers to the foetus, stillbirths, brain damage and extreme physical disabilities became the tragedy of many newborn babes. The effects to future generations cannot be known, not to mention the moral issue of putting short-term profit before the welfare of humans and our precious Earth with its diversity of life.

Thimerosal, a mercury-based preservative used in medications and vaccines, is a topic of concern as it metabolises to ethylmercury and there is no known safe level of exposure to this neurotoxin. Thimerosal has been linked to attention disorders, speech delays, language delays, Tourette Syndrome, misery disorder, seizures, epilepsy, Sudden Infant Death Syndrome, narcolepsy, heart disorders, neurological disorders, asthma and allergies (Kennedy, n.d.). Mercury's synergistic dance with life stressors and metals such as copper, zinc, lead and aluminium (a neurotoxin used as an adjuvant in vaccines) is well documented. Dr Boyd Haley's 2005 paper, *Mercury toxicity: Genetic susceptibility and synergistic effects*, concluded: "The synergistic effects of other heavy metals, diet, antibiotics, etc. on mercury toxicity make it impossible to de-fine a "safe level of mercury exposure." Therefore, it is imperative that we try to eliminate all exposure to mercury; and re-moval from dentistry and medicines is most important and critical to human health."

Future historians will say, "What were they thinking?"

Compact fluorescent lights (CFL's) contain small amounts of mercury. When moving into the home I am now in, I replaced these bulbs and a friend took them to a hardware store for disposal. He came back smiling over the antics of the person he gave them to who said they break all the time and nothing happens. A plastic bag will not contain mercury, sweeping or vacuuming it up is dangerous and if a CFL bulb is broken indoors, a strict procedure is recommended when cleaning up (www.epa. gov/cfl/cleaning-broken-cfl). The question is, "How do we safely dispose of large quantities and reverse environmental pollution that was not a problem for our ancestors when mercury was safely contained within the earth?"

When suffering from chronic fatigue in the 1990's, no general practitioner could help except to offer an antidepressant, which I declined. However, within a short time of seeing an orthomolecular doctor I recovered after following a strict regime of natural supplements, diet and having my amalgams removed. When our immune system is compromised, the body is not able to handle the problems these dentistry issues may present.

Years later, when my dentist sold her practice, the first thing the new dentist did was to whip out one of my wisdom teeth. We had a retail outlet at the time and the next day I was serving customers with tears dripping. It was like turning on a tap that would not stop. The naturopath I was seeing at the time happened to pop in and put her reluctant husband behind the counter. However, within minutes, the poor chap was rescued. Using kinesiology, she took me to the place the kinesiologist did in the session before my chemotherapy treatment, to when my grandmother had passed over. The emotion held in the tooth area of the body was released within minutes and the tears stopped, just like turning off a tap. This makes sense when you know that the wisdom tooth was connected to the heart meridian.

Our healing journey is like creating a work of art and all we can do is to take one step at a time, allowing bodily symptoms to be our guide. We are not bits and pieces operating every which way but an energetic being with the wisdom to heal and function as one organic whole. Four years after my cancer diagnosis, I found and worked with a holistic dentist offering the latest technology from Germany. Gum disease and two infected teeth have now been healed without the trauma so often associated with modern dentistry. The difference in my energy levels and health following this work is noticeable and I believe this to be another step forward on my healing journey.

CHAPTER 18

Earth Therapy

*"As human beings, the realm we have the most
immediate control over is the material.
The physical body is the foundation upon
which our consciousness is based.
Thus, when faced with a restraint
of any sort, we naturally start from the beginning
- with daily diet and lifestyle practices,
which profoundly affect all aspects of our being."*

(Michio Kushi, 1991)

GROUNDING/EARTHING

Scientists are beginning to understand that the earth is a powerful healer. When the skin touches the earth, free electrons that have an antioxidant effect are absorbed into the body. These can neutralise an excess of free radicals that are a by-product of the body's metabolic process and play a role in maintaining health. Today, however, the body finds it difficult to cope with free radical overload due to many factors including nuclear radiation, medical diagnostic equipment, microwaves, electromagnetic fields and environmental chemicals. The oxidation of artificial fat substitutes such as hydrogenated vegetable oils and toxins such as fluoride and chlorine found in drinking water, contribute to the problem. People in past cultures did not have these concerns and wore leather type foot wear, slept close to the earth cocooned within her heart beat and so were grounded and balanced.

When in a meditative state, our brain waves resonate on the same frequency as the earth's electromagnetic field and when connecting to the earth, the chaotic sea of energy we are continually bombarded with is transformed by nature's wisdom. Symptoms of not being grounded can include feeling angry, frustrated, rejected, light headed, anxious or mentally mulling over past events. Walking barefoot on the earth and touching the living soil with your hands can be ways of staying grounded when consuming a raw food diet or spending lots of time in meditation. If connection with the earth is not possible, wear red socks as colours vibrate at different frequencies and red resonates to the part of us that connects to earth.

To support an antioxidant rich diet, that is eating living food, ten minutes of daily contact with the earth to absorb her powerful brand of natural antioxidants can be an important facet of the personal diamond of health. Earthing is scientifically known to bring the stress hormone cortisol into balance, to reduce inflammation, support immunity and to enhance sound sleep essential for health and wellbeing. Barefoot contact with the earth after hopping off an aeroplane can work wonders for softening jet lag woes and can also assist to protect against electromagnetic fields. After running a marathon, take off those sweaty shoes, step onto the earth to accelerate recovery and relieve muscle tension.

Walking on sand, swimming in the ocean, allowing a tinkling brook to flow over your feet or sitting in your garden with bare feet touching the earth are wonderful ways to assist the body to maintain a state of balance. Free electrons abound in salt water and when spending time near the sea the four elements, air, earth, sun and water combine to bring about healing.

It was Leonardo de Vinci who said that the foot is a masterpiece of engineering and a work of art. The foot contains an intricate network of nerve and acupuncture points. Applying pressure to a part of the foot to free blocked energy and bring relief to another part of the body is well documented. This is known as reflexology used by many ancient cultures such as the Indian, Chinese, Egyptian and North and South American healers. Mother Earth is a wonderful reflexologist, so take off those high heels and synthetic shoes, walk barefoot and allow her to do what she loves, work on your body to bring healing and balance.

HELIOTHERAPY

The sun wakens the sleeping earth each morning with gentle fingers of light. This first hour of the dawning is known as an hour of power, a time to yawn, stretch and greet the day with gratitude for our lives. When breathing in the red and orange hues our bodies are awakened, strengthened and revitalised in preparation for a new adventure.

Surya is the Sanskrit name for the sun known to the enlightened sages of past ages as the bringer of life and a symbol of spiritual consciousness. It was known that a daily period of sunbathing gives potent therapeutic benefits for a wide range of degenerative diseases. Today, we have been sadly misguided and overuse sunscreens often containing harmful chemicals that block the ultraviolet rays the skin needs to produce Vitamin D. Physician, scientist and author, Dr Sharon Moalem (2008, p 52) says Vitamin D is a critical component of human biochemistry and points out that Vitamin D deficiency has been shown to play a role in the development of dozens of diseases - everything from many different cancers to diabetes, heart disease, arthritis, psoriasis and mental illness. He says, "Without enough vitamin D, adults are prone to osteoporosis and children are prone to a disease called rickets that results in improper bone growth and deformity." I had rickets as a child and have memories of Poppy putting my legs in callipers every night. Another memory is of the daily dose of Scott's Emulsion (cod liver oil) from the bottle displaying the man with the fish.

Traditional Chinese Medicine advocates the best way to receive the sun's healing benefits is by direct skin and safe eye exposure. Scientists say that when the light from the sun enters the body through the eyes, the pituitary gland and the pineal gland are activated, assisting in the regulation of body functions such metabolism, immunity and endocrine balance. Spending long days indoors under artificial lighting and the prolonged wearing of sunglasses can contribute to pituitary dysfunction. For example, when the body is exposed to the rays from the sun, signals are sent through the optic nerve to the pituitary gland to begin the process of producing more melanin to protect from burning. However, when wearing sunglasses this process is hampered and sunburn may result.

I am not saying precautions are not necessary, but by embracing the sun, earth, air and water therapies we will access nature's healing regime by tuning us into the earth's pulse, our true rhythm. I bathed my children on an open verandah, exposing their bodies to small amounts of sun when possible as it is important to gradually build exposure. They grew into healthy youngsters spending days in the sun due to swimming club commitments and I contribute this in part to the health they enjoy today. It is said that twenty minutes to half an hour per day exposing as much skin as possible is a good recipe for health, although exposure time does vary depending on skin colour, season and location.

If physically connecting to nature is not possible, visualisation techniques can be an effective alternative (see Grounding Visualisation - Chapter 27). Remember Mary who freed her personal inner space from the confines of a hospital bed by taking her mind to a place of beauty in nature where those imaginary free electrons flooded her body, bringing peace and balance. The mind is a powerful tool.

Forest Bathing

Shinrin-yoku or forest bathing is a science studied for many years in Japan. It is regarded as preventative medicine because it has been shown that spending time in a forest environment has a positive effect on our body-mind experience. Just being in such a place with awareness, known as mindful forest therapy, is a de-stressor and can benefit heart rate, blood pressure and blood flow to the brain. Trees release aromatic chemicals said to have anti-cancer properties and spending time in such an environment can boost the immune system. The effects can last for up to one week.

When visiting a forest setting, have an awareness of nature's pharmacopeia and know that within its pages lies the secret to eliminating the sludge from modern living. Nature's library holds a treasure trove of information, every tree a book of knowledge, each leaf a wise word, if only we had the ears to hear and the eyes to see.

CHAPTER 19

Electromagnetic Frequency Pollution

*"I have no doubt in my mind that at
the present time the greatest
polluting element in the earth's environment is the
proliferation of electromagnetic fields."*

(Nobel Prize nominee Dr. Robert O. Becker
author of *Cross Currents* and *The Body Electric,*
interview with Linda Moulton Howe - 2000)

S ince the introduction of electricity, electromagnetic fields (EMF'S) not found in nature and powerful enough to override the earth's natural rhythm, blanket the planet. These have an impact on human energy fields by upsetting the cellular electromagnetic frequency balance and thereby contribute to physical and mental health problems. Artificial electromagnetic fields such as radio wave and microwave frequencies, ex-rays and gamma rays contribute to this energy pollution. Just as the dark region of the moon remains hidden with secrets yet to be told, electricity that has transformed nearly every aspect of our lives also hides a dark side that is not on most people's radar. A willingness to look at the emerging scientific facts and implement appropriate safety precautions is now a challenge if we are to leave a better world for those who follow in our footsteps.

HEALTH CONSIDERATIONS

Electro-hypersensitivity (EHS) is the modern term used for those suffering from the ill effects to electromagnetic frequency exposure. Everyone is affected to varying degrees, especially those living in industrial or urban areas. Airline personnel, medical practitioners spending time in high-tech operating rooms and people working in the electronics industries are examples of those who complain of symptoms such as immune deficiency syndrome, chronic fatigue, hypersensitivity, allergies, headaches, dizziness, mood imbalance and insomnia. Symptoms can be subtle and many do not realise that the wireless technologies in their home, or in their neighbours' homes, could be triggering the problem. EHS is officially recognised as a functional disability in Sweden, where it is intensively researched and the findings are brought to the awareness of the public.

An example is the 2011 Electromagnetic Health.org media advisory of the Seletun Scientific Statement, documenting the findings of seven scientists from five countries and based on a large and growing body of science showing the biological effects of electromagnetic frequencies. It says the combined effect of cell phones, cordless phones, cell towers, WI-FI and wireless internet place billions of people around the world at risk for cancer, neurological disease and reproductive and developmental impairments. Children and pregnant women are a particular concern and new biologically-based public exposure standards are urgently needed to protect public health. The report expresses very great concern for long-term cellular and DNA damage, and the consequences of these exposures to fertility and the health of future generations.

Dr Neil Cherry (1946-2003) was an associate professor of Environmental Health at Lincoln University in New Zealand who extensively researched and lectured on the effects of electromagnetic frequencies on the human body. His work explored many facets of the darker side to electromagnetic fields such as an increased risk of childhood leukemia in relation to residential power lines, domestic wiring and electrical appliances. His report, *Evidence that Electromagnetic fields from high voltage powerlines and in buildings, are hazardous to human health, especially to young children*, showed that those living near and workers maintaining powerlines and substations, are at risk of serious health effects. Dr Cherry believed electromagnetic fields to be genotoxic and carcinogenic and therefore need to be strongly minimised to reduce serious health effects. In 2011, the World Health Organisation classified wireless radiofrequency as a possible human carcinogen. This applies significantly to low-intensity frequency emitting devices such as cell and cordless phones, wireless laptops, electronic baby monitors, wireless classroom access points and wireless antenna facilities.

The Kaiser Permanente Northern California Division of Research issued a press release in 2011 of a study by Drs De-Kun Li, Hong Chen and Rowana Odouli. This is the first study of its kind to associate electromagnetic frequency contact during pregnancy with an increased risk of childhood asthma. Previous research found that magnetic fields - generated typically by power lines and appliances such as microwave ovens, hair dryers and vacuum cleaners - could lead to miscarriage, poor semen quality, immune disorders, and certain type of cancers. Kaiser state, "The prevalence of asthma has been steadily rising since the 1980s, making it the most common chronic condition among children."

What will be the cost to future generations if we remain uneducated as to the dangers of the EMF soup we swim in and subject children to, especially during those vulnerable growing years? Another concern is children's use of iPads when placed on their laps and the lack of awareness of the possible consequences, such as infertility issues occurring in later life.

It is known that some people can develop cross-reactions to chemicals and artificial electromagnetic frequencies, suffering allergic reactions to different frequencies they can also develop chemical allergies. Symptoms include rashes, nausea, dizziness, headaches, light and sound sensitivity, difficulty in concentration, vision disturbances and debilitating fatigue. Award winning journalist, B. Blake Levitt (2007, p 185) warns that continued exposure may result in sensitivity not previously experienced. Symptoms can escalate to debilitating fatigue, depression, decreased memory, sleep disturbances, unusual behaviour and convulsions, perhaps disappearing in time when exposure is addressed. Ms Levitt writes about an interesting development that may bring further understanding. Large numbers of veterans from the Persian Gulf War are experiencing symptoms similar to those mentioned above. Veterans' wives are documented to be suffering the same effects as well as reproductive difficulties and increased miscarriages. Chronic health problems and an increase in birth defects are seen in children conceived after the veteran's return. Chemical toxicity and electromagnetic fields used in modern warfare are thought to be contributory factors.

The BioInitiative 2012

This report examines exposure from electromagnetic fields and wireless technologies such as mobile and cordless phones, smart meters, wireless laptops and routers and baby monitors. The BioInitiative is a result of the combined work of twenty-nine independent scientists and health experts from ten countries. It is an update on a report published in 2007 and covers thirty years of scientific studies linking cancer and electromagnetic field exposure, stating that since 2007, there is more evidence of risk to health affecting billions of people. A recommendation is that wireless and electromagnetic frequency exposure for people with autism disorders, children of all ages, people planning to have a baby and during pregnancy, should be minimised until further research is carried out. A real concern is the link between mobile phone radiation and brain tumors, infertility issues and neurological and autoimmune disease.

It is suggested that as adequate safety standards for protection against electromagnetic frequencies and wireless exposures are not in place, people need to be proactive to protect themselves from these dangers.

Cordless Telephones

Cordless telephones, especially the later models with higher radio frequencies, and mobile phones are now associated with disorders such as brain tumours, eye problems and significant long-term cognitive decline in children. When held close to the head, radiation can suppress the pineal gland's production of melatonin, a hormone responsible for the regulation of the body's circadian rhythm associated with good quality sleep (regeneration occurs during this time), memory and learning. A deficiency of melatonin is associated with arthritis, depression, suicidal tendencies, seasonal affective disorder, miscarriage, schizophrenia, Alzheimer's and Parkinson's disease. Oestrogen balance can be disrupted, adding to the breast cancer risk.

Dr Neil Cherry (2002) researched and strongly suggested that exposure to these frequencies disrupts the delicate balance of the brain's electro-chemical communications. The imbalance of minerals such as calcium and neurotransmitters such as serotonin, caused by mobile phones, associated with altered mood resulting in depression, suicide, rage, and violence. Radio and microwave frequency at low residential exposure levels associated with sleep disruption, depression, chronic fatigue, headaches, impaired memory and learning, still births, cot deaths, accelerated aging, premature births and birth deformities.

It is recognised that children and teenagers are particularly vulnerable, having a greater sensitivity to frequencies because the absorption of electromagnetic energy in a young person's head is much higher than that of an adult. Countries such as Germany, India, the United Kingdom, Israel, Finland and Belgium are calling for precautionary measures to limit children's mobile phone use. In Russia, where human exposure to EMF radiation has been extensively studied for over fifty years, it is recommended that pregnant women along with children under eighteen years avoid using a mobile phone. In 2012, the Electromagnetic Health. org published a press release in which Professor Yury Grigoriev who is chairman of the Russian National Committee on Non-ironising Radiation Protection, calls for the world to listen. He states, "The brain is a critical organ. Vital brain structures are under EMF exposure daily when using a mobile phone. The brain is made up of permanent complex biophysical processes and vital functions. We need to take care with mobile phones and use distance and reduce time. Children should use mobile phones for emergencies only and also use hands free."

The BioInitiative 2012 Report found that public safety limits do not seem to be sufficiently protective of public health, particularly for the young (embryo, foetus, neonate and the very young child). It states,

"Fetal (in utero) and early childhood exposures to cell phone radiation and wireless technologies in general may be a risk factor for hyperactivity, learning disorders and behavioral problems in school. There is good evidence to suggest that many toxic exposures to the fetus and very young child have especially detrimental consequences depending on when they occur during the critical phases of growth and development (time windows of critical development), where such exposures may lay the seeds of health harm that develops even decades later."

I am saddened to know that during the time when a child is most vulnerable, safe within the mother's womb, unseen frequencies can interfere with its development and with ongoing exposure can become a heart-rending experience for the child and family.

Everyday Exposure

Examples of everyday exposure to electromagnetic frequency fields are:

*   Electric blankets and electrically heated waterbeds emit a field above safe levels and subject the whole body to close exposure. Pregnant woman who use them are known to experience a higher than normal rate of miscarriage (Levitt, 2007, p 161).
*   Electric razors generate fields creating a long-term risk to the brain.
*   Multiple rows of fluorescent lights found in offices and school rooms subject everyone in the room to over exposure.
*   Computers, fax machines, printers and photo copiers.
*   Compact fluorescent lights (CFL's) contribute to dirty electricity which is a potential carcinogen, generate high magnetic fields and contain mercury. CFL's are known to cause symptoms such as dizziness, migraines, fatigue and anxiety by those with electromagnetic frequency sensitivity.
*   Ideally the bedroom should be free of electromagnetic frequency exposure from appliances such as televisions, mobile phones, personal computers and electric clocks that may be situated near

the head while sleeping. Electricity meter boxes emit frequencies not stopped by walls and should be placed away from a sleeping area.

In the November/December 2014 issue of Alternative Therapies in Health and Medicine, Dr Federica Lamech, an Australian physician, published the first medical study of people reporting symptoms to smart meters. Symptoms included insomnia, headaches, tinnitus, fatigue, cognitive disturbances, dysesthesias and dizziness. As electro-hypersensitivity syndrome (EHS) was not reported by those taking part in the study prior to exposure to wireless meters, it was concluded that smart meters may have unique characteristics that lower people's threshold for symptom development.

Residential magnetic fields from power transmission lines and incorrect wiring configurations can affect the home. Dr Dietrich Klinghart says, "Our homes do not breathe, they build up toxic chemicals and they permit electromagnetic radiation to come in. By the time a person moves into a new home it is already moldy. Most U.S. children grow up in homes that are toxic or electromagnetically contaminated. Adults present with loss of zest, short-term memory loss, lack of creativity, sex drive and potency, insomnia, fatigue, dulling of the senses, and a dramatic increase in neurological and psychiatric illnesses" (Greenberg, 2007).

Dr Mercola in his article, *Why Did the Russians Ban Microwave Appliances Found in 90% of Americans Homes*, writes that Dr Hans Ulrich Hertel was the first scientist, along with Dr Bernard Blanc of the Swiss Federal Institute of Technology and the University Institute for Biochemistry, to conduct a quality clinical study on the effects of microwaved ingredients on the blood and the human body. Dr Hertel fought for many years to have his findings concerning the dangers of microwave ovens acknowledged. A 'gag' order was issued by the Swiss Courts in response to findings that food cooked or defrosted in a microwave oven can cause changes in the blood similar to the process found in a developing carcinoma. Other studies indicate that microwave ovens can leak electromagnetic radiation and can convert food cooked in it to carcinogenic substances. The nutritional value of plant food that supports the immune system to ensure good health was found to be diminished.

The Age of Electricity

Donna Fisher (2009, p 105) says, "The age of electricity, which has changed our lives dramatically, both industrially and personally, and allowed us to live virtual twenty-four-hour days has contributed significantly to death and serious disease." Research, she writes, points to the parallel rise in the disease spectrum we are seeing today.

Dirty electricity, a term used for radiofrequency voltage peaks and harmonics generated from electrical wiring, is also a concern to general health. This is particularly the case in areas where a lot of time is spent sleeping, as it can radiate up to two meters from source. Ms Fisher (2009, p 107) tells us, "As a major contributor to the cancer story, dirty electricity is the largest threat to our health that we have ever faced, as it is very much a part of our daily lives. It is in our homes, our workplaces, our schools and our hospitals. It is everywhere. This dirty electricity plague is bigger than all of us." It is wise to do your own research to find a proven system suitable to your requirements in order to clean the electricity lived with on a daily basis.

Donna Fisher's books, *Silent Fields* and *More Silent Fields*, are well sourced, easy to read and highly recommended. Nalani was visiting, having spent Christmas on one of the small islands in the Solomon group. *Silent Fields* was on the coffee table and after a quick browse, was so interested she read it before leaving the following morning.

"You know," she said, "there's little EMF exposure on the island I visited."

I loved hearing the stories of a way of living where everything is shared, of the week-long Christmas festivities, sending laughter to ripple through bodies soaked in nature's four elements, fire, earth, air and water. The stories of fresh fish caught and cooked with reverence and of children who are safe to roam, their bare feet drawing in nature's secrets. Here fruit, free from chemical sprays, falls from tree into grateful hands and there is a togetherness that is only an echo in the remembrance of Western society.

Nalani commented that she knew of no mental illness on this island - bipolar disorder, schizophrenia, attention deficit disorder and the list of 'disorders' that have now been invented and labelled are unknown.

Nalani, a Solomon Islander, has often visited. I remember witnessing her concern when seeing tantrum-throwing children that is often the case in our society. She said this was never the case in the Solomon Islands and indeed, her children have an inner peace I have rarely seen in Western youngsters.

I was interested to hear her comment that there is no word for 'stress' in her native dialogue.

On the small island where Nalani was born there are no televisions, where cartoon characters such as the deplorable Homer Simpson set the dinner scene, no movie theatres where the antics of the Dark Knight trigger many a nightmare. Video games, teaching children the art of modern warfare, are not a part of their culture. However, since writing this, Nalani tells me that mobile phone towers have now been installed and mobile phones are becoming a common commodity. It will be interesting to see in years to come if a lifestyle echoing those of her ancestors will be sufficient to counteract risk factors associated with mobile phone use, such as learning and memory problems, increased irritability, sleep and stress disorders.

Nalani believes tribal connectedness to be a key to good physical, emotional and mental health, saying everyone is cared for in her culture, especially the young and the elderly. Aged homes where the elders are put to graze are nowhere to be seen, the aged are revered and lead a relatively healthy, drug-free lifestyle to the end of their days. Before the infiltration of Western influence into the Solomon way of life, this was always the case with people living to a healthy one hundred plus years. Loneliness is not a word in this culture, nor is suicide. Nalani says we are here for a short time and it is our everyday choices that matter, for these have an impact on the future children. How right she is. Human social genomics, the study of how everyday life circumstances influence human gene expression, says social environmental conditions have been found to associate with how certain genes are expressed. The generational impact of these changes to our DNA is now not a new concept.

Cancer, mental health issues and brain disorders to name but a few are running rampant throughout the world. I believe small changes matter and that knowledge is vital to regaining health and preventing disease. We live in an environment swimming in electromagnetic frequencies and a growing number of scientific voices are saying that we have a serious problem on our hands. Power and big dollars have silenced many, the hour is late and we must seriously consider the consequences of remaining uninformed. When dealing with chronic illness there may be lower tolerance to exposure and making small changes such as keeping mobile phones away from the body, unplugging electrical appliances when not in use and discarding electric blankets, can make a difference. We do not know what level of exposure over a period of time is safe, if any.

What are we going to say to our children and grandchildren down the track when they ask, "What did you do when …?"

CHAPTER 20

Chemicals in our Food

*"We are told these chemicals are safe, but the toxic
smorgasbord of chemicals used by many commercial farmers
has unintended and undesirable side effects, including
poisoning the soil, water and soil micro-organism."*

(Buckley, 2010)

The body has an amazing ability to heal and maintain optimum health given a supportive environment. What we choose to put into our body is one of the most important decisions we will make towards the quality of our lives. However, a problem today is our lack of knowledge as to the quality of our food. Supermarkets are packed with brightly coloured produce and shelving laden with enticing packets, tins and jars of every variety of food imaginable. When I say to people that there is little life-giving food in supermarkets, I am looked at strangely, ignored or they say, "I eat okay."

Do they? I do not believe so and here is why.

Unless specified organic, vegetables and fruit are grown with toxic pesticides, herbicides and artificial fertilisers. Produce can be sprayed with petroleum products to keep it looking fresh and shiny. Irradiating food is a method used to destroy contaminants and to make it last longer so as to transport it worldwide. However, this process has been shown to destroy essential nutrients and can produce toxic chemical compounds such as formaldehyde, formic acid, quinines and benzene.

Chemical pesticides, herbicides and fungicides are linked to the epidemic of diseases we are experiencing today. Most crops farmed by conventional methods use large quantities of these toxic substances. Bev Buckley (2010, pp 21-22), a farmer with over twenty-five years' experience in training and educating, writes, "More than 7,200 registered biocide products are used in Australia. There is virtually no testing to detect the residues of poison in our food and little research has been done to determine safe intake levels, if indeed any level is safe." She warned that most agriculture poisons leave residues of breakdown chemicals when they degrade and in some cases become even more toxic as they break down. It is Ms Buckley's opinion that the epidemic of diseases we are seeing today is caused by this pollution and the solution is not more man-made drugs, but in growing healthy nutrient-rich food. Quality has been forgotten in industrial farming methods, producing large quantities of food but leading to soil erosion, desertification and loss of soil fertility. 'Living' soil once containing billions of microbes, bacteria, worms and fungi, is now becoming dead soil.

The effects that pesticides are having on children's health is a growing concern. It has been found that parental exposure can affect children before conception, during gestation or after birth. The Pesticide Action Network North America (PANNA) published a report in 2012 called *A Generation in Jeopardy: how pesticides are undermining our children's health and intelligence*. It is a review of scientific studies on the impact of pesticides on children's health, saying that children today are sicker than they were a generation ago and names pesticides as one key driver of this sobering trend. Exposure, even at a low level in some instances, is now associated with the problems we are seeing today such as childhood cancers, autism, ADHD, obesity, asthma, diabetes, birth defects, delayed neuro-development and impaired cognitive processes.

Supporting farmers who use healthy growing methods, sourcing local farmers' markets and creating kitchen gardens are ways to limit the intake of these chemicals. Our bodies vibrate at certain frequencies and the food we ingest can either assist to maintain a high vibration or lower the scale due to contaminated air, water and soil. Foods that contain toxic elements subject our bodies to physical stress. Polluted soil grows inferior produce, lacking the nutrients we need for health. If the goodness is not in the soil, then it will not be in the fresh-looking broccoli you buy for its promised bounty. Conscious farming methods are the foundation for sustainable living.

"Don't we need pesticides to keep pests away?" you may ask.

The answer is, "No."

Bev Buckley (2010, pp 25-26) says, "Reinstatement of trace elements in our soil eliminates all plant diseases, pest and insect attack. If there are no pests and diseases attacking our plants, we have no need to use toxic agricultural chemicals. The fact that farmers need to use these substances with such frightening frequency is a clear indication that the food they are producing is not healthy." When the quality of the soil is nutrient-rich, the quality of the vegetables and fruit are also nutrient-rich and do not attract pests, insects and diseases that are nature's way of ensuring unhealthy plants do not reproduce. This is true of people and animals as those who are healthy do not become ill.

GENETICALLY MODIFIED FOOD

"Just as we got rid of slavery, we've got to get rid of slavery of life, through patents on seed. We have a higher duty to protect life on earth, to protect biodiversity and to pass on seed to our future." Vandana Shiva - recipient of the Right Livelihood Award, often called, the alternative Nobel Prize - (Mauro, 2013).

Another concern is genetically modified (GM) food. Sitting on those supermarket shelves can be food containing genetically modified corn, canola and soybean of which we may not be aware. When compared to nature's system, Ho (2013) says, "Artificial genetic modification, in contrast, is crude, imprecise, and interferes with the natural process." An unfolding story told by independent research is pointing to adverse effects to health and longevity, the ecosystems that support life and a possible nightmarish legacy being left for generations to come.

Jeffrey Smith, a renowned researcher on the dangers we could be facing when remaining unaware of the long-term consequences, tells the tale in his books, *Genetic Roulette* and *Seeds of Deception*. Smith (2007, p 4) believes the odds are stacked against us if the results from the few laboratory animal feeding safety studies with GMO's are an indication. These results show a long list of adverse effects including potentially precancerous growth in the digestive tract, stunted growth, impaired immunity, bleeding stomachs, altered gene expression, less developed brains and testicles, increased death rates and higher offspring mortality. Jeffrey Smith's is not a solo voice, there are many, such as that of Dr Thierry Vrain, a former pro-GMO scientist and Canadian government spokesperson advocating the safety of GM food. He is now one of the scientific community's leading voices questioning the safety of this aspect of our food supply. Dr Vrain, when speaking on an online GMO summit in 2013, commented that there is plenty of evidence from countries such as Russia, Japan and Europe indicating serious health and environment problems.

Crops can be engineered to be herbicide tolerant, that is to survive a toxic dose of herbicide, to produce their own pesticide, known as pesticide production, or to do both. However, the dark side to this technology is now coming to light, an example being a two-year study conducted by French researchers at the University of Caen on rats fed GM maize containing the herbicide Roundup. This was the first long-term toxicological study ever conducted and the disturbing results showed mass tumors, some larger than golf balls, severe damage to multiple organs and a decreased life expectancy (Seralini et al., 2014).

In 2011, when Dr Mercola interviewed Dr Don Huber, retired professor of plant pathology at Purdue University, he was informed that glyphosate, an active ingredient in Roundup, becomes systemic throughout the plant and cannot be washed off. Dr Huber explained that the chemical is inside the plant and once eaten, ends up in the gut where it can wreak havoc with health as eighty-percent of the immune system lives there and relies on a healthy ratio of good and bad bacteria. Having spent twenty years researching how to reverse the damage caused by glyphosate he believes we must begin now, saying, "When future historians come to write about our era they are not going to write about the tons of chemicals we did or didn't apply. When it comes to glyphosate they are going to write about our willingness to sacrifice our children and to jeopardise our very existence by risking the sustainability of our agriculture; all based upon failed promises and flawed science. The only benefit is that it affects the bottom-line of a few companies. There's no nutritional value."

Dr Stephanie Seneff, a senior scientist at the Massachusetts Institute of Technology, after three decades of research, believes that because of its wide usage, glyphosate may be the most biologically disruptive chemical in our environment. She published a study in 2013 with retired science consultant, Anthony Samsel associating glyphosate's potential to affect biological systems contributing to modern-day diseases such as inflammatory bowel disease, obesity, depression, ADHD, autism, Alzheimer's disease, Parkinson's disease, multiple sclerosis, cancer, cachexia, infertility, and developmental malformations. Glyphosate's negative impact on the body was shown to be insidious, manifesting slowly over time as the resulting inflammation damaged cellular systems. Glyphosate was found to work synergistically with other factors, such as insufficient sun exposure, dietary deficiencies in critical nutrients such as sulphur and zinc, and chemical toxins whose detoxification is impaired by glyphosate.

The adverse impact on the environment and the livelihood of farmers worldwide is becoming evident. Super weeds have built up a resistance to the chemical herbicides used in growing GM foods. India reports a high farmer suicide rate due to financial debt created by drought, lack of government support and failed promises from the multinational companies peddling those GM crops. The assured higher yields have not eventuated due to problems such as soil infertility caused by the use of chemical fertilisers. Nor are these crops drought resistant, as promised.

Our most precious commodity is our farmers. If farmers are not looked after during a time of need, then who will feed the people when the devastation caused by the multinational corporations becomes an insurmountable problem? Andrew Kimbrell (2007, p 63) says, "Containing the GM plague is impossible because wind, rain, birds and other vectors, indiscriminately can carry seeds." He points out, "This pollution of seeds increases risks to conventional farmers and seriously jeopardises the future of organic agriculture."

A growing number of countries, including Russia, Poland, Germany, France, Scotland, Italy, Austria, Greece, Poland, and Belgium require labelling and have restricted or ceased the cultivation and importing of GM foods. For example, Sikkim, situated in the Himalayas, has now become India's first organic state ensuring food security, free from genetically modified, chemically laden produce for its people (Oberst, 2016). Restrictions or bans on glyphosate are now being seen, for example, the Dutch city, Rotterdam, lodged a successful petition called, 'Non-toxic Sidewalks for Our Children' submitted by concerned citizens to ban Roundup (Renter, 2013).

Navdanya, an organisation situated in North India, has evolved from a search for non-violent farming to protect biodiversity, the Earth and small farmers. Founded by scientist and environmentalist, Dr Vandana Shiva, it began as a programme of the Research Foundation for Science, Technology and Ecology (RFSTE). Navdanya promotes chemical free organic agriculture and the awareness of the dangers of genetic engineering. It fights against patents on seeds and plants, standing up for seed sovereignty and people's rights to food and water security. Navdanya says that organic agriculture is not just a source of safer, healthier, tastier food, it is an answer to rural poverty, saving the Earth and the people. Information on Dr Shiva's work can be seen at website: www.navdanya.org.

In 2015, the World Health Organisation declared glyphosate to be a probable human carcinogen and in 2017, California's Environmental Protection Agency (EPA) added glyphosate to its list of chemicals known to cause cancer. Evidence is accumulating to say that genetically modified food crops are dangerous to human health and the environment. When we poison and genetically modify our environment, we poison and genetically modify ourselves. However, voices can now be heard coming from every corner of the Earth saying 'no' to multi-national corporations who are stealing the health, happiness, diversity and the future of the children. People are coming together to form groups aimed at producing local communities that are self-sufficient and working for the benefit of all, not just to give power and profit to the few at the expense of many. Hard work for the good of Earth's family, not the greedy few, will coax life back into the living soil, awakening the hearts of depleted nations. Ancient Japanese wisdom says, "The soil and the people are essentially one."

Food Additives

Food from all over the world sits on those supermarket shelves because chemicals used in the packaging and preserving process enable it to transport distances and prolong shelf life. However, a dark side is emerging with research linking many of these chemicals to disease including cancer.

Food additives give texture, flavour and colour. They are found in junk food, confectionary, soft drinks and in so called 'healthy foods' such as muesli bars, bread, yoghurt and juice. Many are linked to mental health issues such as ADHD and ODD that can open the way for drugging with dangerous chemicals, an issue over which there is much controversy. One psychiatrist who is an advocate for the stopping of psychiatric drugging of children is Dr Peter Breggin, acting medical expert in liability suits often involving adverse drug effects. His peer reviewed articles and published books provide valuable information on topics such as psychiatric drugs in violence and psychiatric drug withdrawal. Dr Breggin's work may be viewed at: www.breggin.org.

Intolerance to food chemicals can contribute to many health issues and the epidemic we are seeing today of learning difficulties and behavioural problems in children. While everyone may be affected, those most susceptible are the young whose immune systems are not fully developed, seniors, people with compromised immune systems and those who eat junk or processed food. Food intolerance can be delayed or build up slowly over time. Artificial food colourings, preservatives, flavour enhancers and sweeteners should be avoided as we do not know the long-term effect of digesting these unnatural chemicals, either by themselves or in combination. Not all of the chemicals in packaged and pre-prepared foods are required to be listed on the label. The only way to know what is in your food is to purchase from reliable sources and grow and prepare from scratch yourself.

Food colourings can be derived from coal tar, an example being tartrazine yellow dye (No. E102), linked to effects such as hyperactivity, behavioural changes in children, migraines, asthma, itching, rhinitis and blurred vision. Tartrazine can be found in many products such as cereal bars, yoghurt, jam, chewing gum, ice cream, fruit juice cordial as well as face paint, crayons, medicines, cosmetics and it is used as a wool and silk dye. It is a possible food carcinogen due to being an azo dye and therefore linked to bladder, prostate, rectum, stomach and ovarian cancers. Symptoms caused by azo dye intoxication include vomiting, nausea, diarrhea, swelling of the mouth, itching, headaches and difficulty breathing (Almeida et al., 2014).

Food colourings can be derived from petroleum, an example being brilliant blue (No E133) which is a synthetic azo dye linked to hyperactivity, asthma, allergic reactions and neurotoxicity. It is often used with tartrazine to form green as in tinned green peas and can be found in sweets, cereal bars, beverages, canned foods, face paint, soap, toothpaste, cosmetics, hair dye and mouthwash. Brilliant blue is a suspected food carcinogen that has been banned in countries such as Belgium, France, Germany, Switzerland, Sweden, Austria and Norway.

There are many food colourings, preservatives and sweeteners and one that is receiving a lot of bad press is the sweetener, Aspartame. Made from aspartic acid, phenylalanine and methanol, Aspartame has been found in over five thousand foods including chewing gum, sugar free foods, vitamins and medicines, including those for children. More than ninety effects have been reported including asthma, seizures, memory loss, mood changes, gradual weight gain, headache, dizziness, insomnia, vomiting, depression and aggression. Reactions can be acute or manifest over a period of time. A study by Soffritti et al. (2006) from the European Ramazzini Foundation of Oncology and Environmental Sciences, Italy, concluded that Aspartame is a multipotential carcinogenic agent, even at a low daily dose, and urgent re-evaluation of the present guidelines on the use and consumption is required.

Retired professor of food science from the Arizona State University and author of *While Science Sleeps*, Dr Woodrow Monte, in his article, *Dangers of Aspartame*, says there is no safe intake level of methanol (an ingredient in aspartame). He writes, "Methanol is particularly dangerous to humans, more so than any other animal. When humans consume low doses of methanol it is metabolised directly into formaldehyde which is a cancer producing agent of the same level of danger as asbestos and plutonium. This conversion does not all happen in the liver, a common misconception, but also in the brain and a woman's breast. It is my belief that diet soda has contributed to the rise of breast cancer and multiple sclerosis that has been preceded by the use of Aspartame as a food ingredient in every country that has allowed its use."

Man-made oestrogen-mimicking food additives, called xenoestrogens (xeno meaning foreign oestrogens that can bind to a cell's oestrogen receptor site), are also a concern. These contribute to hormone related issues such as fibrocystic breast disease, infertility, depression, endometriosis, mood swings, excessive weight gain and breast, ovary, testicular and prostate cancers. They can be found in food due to the use of pesticides, herbicides and fungicides, in plastic containers, pharmaceuticals and meat and dairy when animals are subjected to oestrogenic drugs.

It is wise to become knowledgeable about what is in the food you are buying and have at hand a comprehensive shopping guide such as the one published by Bill Statham and Lindy Schneider called *The Chemical Maze*. This is available from website: www.chemicalmaze.com.

It is estimated that Australians consume approximately sixty to seventy kilogrammes of refined sugar per person each year. It comes from sugar cane or sugar beets, which are processed to extract the sugar which plays a part in the epidemic of modern-day disease and is cancer's favourite food. Sugar, used as a sweetener and a preservative, is known to feed yeast infections, can trigger headaches including migraine, depression, ADHD, antisocial behavior, aggression and the list goes on and on.

A child's behavior, learning ability and attention span can be severely affected when sugar sensitivity is an issue and perhaps sugar is Western society's favourite addiction. Monica Colmsjo (2009, pp 18, 19) says, "It is estimated that as much as seventy-five percent of humans have a genetic sensitivity to refined sugar and a quarter of those are extremely sensitive. If you are sugar sensitive, sugar in all forms, including white flour and white rice, will be as addictive as heroin or morphine - causing cravings that are sometimes stronger than the heroin addicts' cravings." Ms Colmsjo describes sugar as being a drug refined from sugar cane just as cocaine is a drug refined from coca leaves and opium is a drug refined from poppies. When taking high doses of refined sugar your blood sugar levels rise, lifting your mood and energy. However, if your body does not cope with the 'sugar hit', a 'crash' and then a craving for more will follow along with symptoms such as restlessness, agitation and mood swings. Alcohol is a refined sugar, cigarettes are known to contain sugar and pre-disposing children to an excess of sugar-laden foods that can lead to an addiction, may open the way for future substance abuse. It is better to snack on nature's candies such as figs containing phytonutrients, antioxidants and an abundance of vitamins and minerals.

Refined sugar can trigger the inflammation process. Inflammation plays a role in keeping our body in optimum health and can be likened to controlled scrub burning for clearing and rejuvenation. However, when out of control, the resulting fire if intense and ongoing can decimate all within its path resulting in loss and heartache. At the heart of chronic disease is prolonged inflammation and knowing that our food choices can impact this process gives us a valuable tool to overcome genetic and dietary sensitivities. When dealing with chronic illness, it is important to protect the body from as many stressors as possible in order to support its potential to heal.

PROCESSED AND FAST FOOD

We have not taken a wise pathway trusting food manufacturers to bring to our children's table the abounding health promised on those cardboard boxes, television screens and in glossy magazine advertisements.

Processed and fast foods contain little, if any, health value and can be a toxic cocktail of artificial colourings, flavourings, preservatives, refined sugar, aspartame, monosodium glutamate (MSG) and more. Studies on fast food consumption and health are slowly coming to light, an example being Ellwood et al. (2013) and the global findings from the International Study of Asthma and Allergies in Childhood (ISAAC) Phase Three. Results showed that fast food consumption, three times per week for 13-14-year-old adolescents and 7-6-year-old children, was associated with an increased risk of severe asthma and/or severe rhino conjunctivitis and eczema. However, including fruit and vegetables in the diet three times per week, was associated with a potential protective effect against severe asthma.

I will never forget the day I was on a road trip with Deb and Cleveland and we stopped at a fast food restaurant for breakfast. All major highways have detours to these outlets and at the time of writing it is not easy to find healthy food restaurants when travelling.

Wondering what I was going to eat and amazed to see the place buzzing with people, I asked, "What are they doing here at this hour in the morning?"

"Eating breakfast," was the reply.

Eating breakfast!

"Eating breakfast,'" Cleveland repeated, reading the look on my face.

These obese people should never be in here, my inner critic offered in judgmental disgust.

I remember the feeling of aloneness hovering over that large barn-like place they call a restaurant, on the dawning of a new day. Where was the awareness of the sun's rising rays touching everything with a drop of life-giving light to awaken humans, animals and plants alike? I searched for a sign of family togetherness and for wholesome food to give nourishment to bodies eager to explore another day. I searched for a flicker of gratitude, even animation on the bland faces eating the bland food. There was none.

CHAPTER 21

First Line Breast Screening

*"The causes of cancer are already known.
Toxic diets, toxic lifestyles, toxic environments, toxic drug
treatments, and toxic diagnostic techniques cause cancer."*

(Dr Sherrill Sellman, 2003)

I know that it is wise to take control of my own health which means having access to the latest information, believing in the healing methods I choose and listening to my inner guidance and my body. I have learned the importance of integrating positive lifestyle changes to lessen the chances of breast cancer recurring. I believe it is wise to research the pros and cons before subjecting my body to further diagnostic tests as imposing stressors on a system weakened by cancer and chemotherapy requires careful consideration. I understand that it is important to have regular tactile breast checks and a first line breast screening method such as mammography, thermography or computerised breast imaging. I know these do not diagnose but point the way to further investigation such as a needle biopsy, ultrasound or MRI. Breast examinations and tests, however, can be misleading and although I was having a regular physical breast examination with a clinical nurse, the tumour in my right breast was not detected. It was the messages received from my body that prompted further investigation. Knowledge is power, prevention is wise and body wisdom is perhaps our most formidable ally.

Mammography

The efficacy of this technology is now being questioned. Breast tissue, especially in premenopausal women, is highly sensitive to ionising radiation which is utilised in CT scans, ex-rays and mammograms. Research has shown that ionising radiation damage to genes is cumulative and there is no safe level of exposure, adding to the risk of developing a malignancy or genetic disease. Professor Michael Baum, emeritus professor of surgery at University College, London and a former supporter of mammogram breast screening, is now an advocate for scrapping this procedure especially in premenopausal women. The scientific landscape is rapidly changing and this is aptly expressed by Professor Baum when being interviewed by Maryann Napoli in 2002. He said, "Scientific truths are only temporary expressions of reality that serve us for the time. There's no such thing as scientific truth. It's all an approximation to reality. A true scientist has to accept that his version of reality will be overturned in the fullness of time. If you can't accept that, you're not a scientist."

Voices from the medical and scientific community can be heard warning of over-diagnosis, over-treatment and pain from breast compression that can cause the rupture of small blood vessels leading to the spreading of malignant cells. Other factors to consider are the dangers of ironising radiation exposure contributing to mutations that can lead to disease. The vulnerability of women carrying a BRCA gene mutation to radiation-induced cancer is also a concern. This is a tumour suppressor gene and when functioning normally can assist to repair DNA damage but can mutate due to radiation and environmental toxin exposure.

The Cochrane data base has long been a place where doctors go to review objective information compiled by an independent group of international scientists. In 2001, Cochrane published a review on mammography mass screening in The Lancet and The Cochrane Library. It reported over-diagnosis (estimated to be approximately fifty percent), over-use of aggressive treatment including increased mastectomies and no evidence of increased survival benefit for breast cancer. Professor

Peter Gotzsche, director of the Nordic Cochrane Centre, commented on the updated review published in 2011 saying that whilst this information may have been considered controversial in 2001, it is now increasingly being recognised to be true even by those who supported the introduction of screening. Cochrane published a leaflet, updated in 2012, informing women of the benefits and the harms and this can be viewed at: www. nordic.cochrane.org/mammography-screening-leaflet.

Samuel Epstein (2013, pp 49, 60), professor emeritus of the environmental public health and occupational medicine at the University of Illinois School of Public Health and chairman of the Cancer Prevention Coalition, states: "Women should be informed of their ex-ray exposure and individual and cumulative risks each time they undergo mammography. The coalition should demand an immediate ban on obsolete high-dose ex-ray equipment and the abandonment of routine mammograms on premenopausal women." Professor Epstein reminds us that the late Dr John Gofman (1918-2007), professor emeritus of molecular and cell biology at the University of California, published an analysis in his classic 1995 book, *Preventing Breast Cancer*, stressing that medical radiation is probably the single most important cause of the modern breast cancer epidemic.

"But, it's all we have," I have been told. Not true, while mammography may be a favourite tool of the Western medical system, in countries such as Japan, France, Sweden and Germany a gentler, safer means of detecting early breast cancers is more widely used.

Thermography

This is known as thermography, a form of thermal (infrared) imaging that has been FDA approved in the United States of America since 1982. This technology is said to be able to detect a cancer, eight to ten years before it would be discovered by mammography or physical examination, no rays enter the body and there is no pain or compression of the breasts. Another benefit is that it is not dependent upon tissue density which can be an issue with mammogram technology. Thermography detects subtle temperature change in the breast that may or may not be cancer.

A mammogram detects a mass that has already formed but by this time, a tumour may have been growing for at least seven years (this is not early detection). To my way of thinking, it is valuable to be able to detect a change in breast tissue before the arrival of lumps and bumps. Dr Galina Migalka, a pioneer in non-invasive diagnostic medical imaging, combines thermography, ultrasound and bio-electro scanning to detect disease in the early stages. Lifestyle changes can then be made to correct the imbalance and ongoing monitoring, using thermography, carried out to see what is working. For further information on Dr Migalka's work, see website: www.universalmedicalimaging.com.

Computerised Breast Imaging

Computerised breast imaging has many benefits. Sensors are not confused by dense breast tissue, scars or implants, small breasts are easily scanned and it is a non-invasive, pain and radiation free system. Approved by the Therapeutic Goods Administration (TGA) in Australia and cleared by the United States Food and Drug Administration for documenting the Clinical Breast Exam it is used in countries such as India, China and Turkey for general screening. This new technology that was developed in the United States of America and known as the Sure Touch Visual Mapping System has research to show a ninety-four percent accuracy in identifying malignant lesions (Kaufman et al., 2006).

CHAPTER 22

Green Chemistry - A Future Vision

*"One must know which diseases are caused by natural
forces and which are caused by material elements."*

Hippocrates
(Reid, 2003, p 75)

What was thought to be the first documentation of occupational cancer, saying chimney sweeps exposed to soot had a tendency to develop cancer of the scrotum, was published by an English physician Percival Pott in 1775. Environmental cancer was studied and recorded in the early twentieth century, for example in 1915, Japanese pathologists at Tokyo University induced skin cancer in laboratory animals by putting coal tar on the ears of rabbits. In 1935, experiments were carried out showing that if particular dyes were ingested, liver cancer could occur in rabbits (Fox, 1991).

Dr Devra Davis (2007, p 91) said, "The Germans had understood much about the ways various toxic agents kill people quickly and cause permanent damage that leads to death more slowly." She tells us that Nazi Germany had documented information on the link between chemical compounds and cancer but when translated into English and taken to the executives of the companies involved in the United States, this information was downplayed. Findings on cancer-causing agents in the workplace carried out by scientists working for companies producing

130

these toxic chemicals, met with the same fate. The heart of big business was not concerned with the welfare of its workers. Perhaps history will record that this disregard contributed to the formation of another business machine, the cancer industry.

However, the concept that chemicals can be carcinogenic is coming into everyday consciousness. Chemicals known to be carcinogenic can be found in face creams, make-up, lipsticks, shampoos, conditioners, toothpaste, deodorants, mouth wash and baby products to name but a few. Sitting on those chemist and department store shelves are products promising health, beauty and youth and containing chemicals about which we know little of the toxic effects. These harmful ingredients can find their way into the blood stream via the skin which is extremely absorbent. They enter by the back door, so to speak, by-passing the detoxifying pathways in the liver.

Journalist and writer specialising in environmental issues, Elizabeth Grossman (2009, p 4) writes, "While not acutely toxic at levels routinely encountered, it appears that even at low levels some of these compounds can disrupt normal cell function with a number of disturbing outcomes. Among these impacts is interference with endocrine system hormones and genetic mechanisms that regulate reproductive and neurological development and metabolism." The aim of green chemistry is to eliminate risk at the design stage and to assist in solving environmental issues. However, this has not happened to date but is a vision for the future. Once in our bodies, chemicals that may be carcinogenic, can pass from one generation to the next through the umbilical cord and the breast milk. Irreversible birth defects and other health problems due to chemical exposure at the time a child is slumbering within the womb or during the early growing years is now on the scientific radar.

IS MY LIPSTICK SAFE?

I often hear, "It wouldn't be on the market if it wasn't safe."

Researcher, health advocate and author, Jean McDonald-Smith (2011) found that chemists creating products for our homes and families have little or no training in long-term toxicology or environmental science.

The possible damage to future generations is not known as limited requirements are in place for testing ingredients for safety to humans, animals and the environment. Nor are there appropriate protocols in place for labelling products known to be carcinogenic, allergenic or that pose a toxic threat. A product can be labelled organic, natural or green but this does not mean that chemicals classified as being toxic or hazardous are not present. Not all of the ingredients are listed and many have never undergone safety testing. It is wise to do your own research and to become aware of what is in the products you purchase.

The late biochemist, Dr Hulda Clark (1993, p 149) said that not a single one can be continued when dealing with chronic illness because they are full of toxic substances. Dr Clark advised against the use of commercial salves, ointments, lotions, colognes, perfumes, massage oils, deodorant, mouthwash, toothpaste, even when the labels say 'herbal' or 'natural'. She advocated the removal of chemical cleaning products from the home and said that paints, varnishes, insect sprays and herbicides should be stored in a shed separate from the house as chemical fumes can enter the house from an attached garage.

WHAT WOULD OUR WILDLIFE SAY?

Are we considering the cruelty to animals and environmental pollution when dealing with the disposal of these chemicals? If we had the ears to hear what would our wildlife say? What stories would the trees, plants, waterways, creeks and bubbling brooks have to tell of our diminishing pristine natural world? Would we hear tales of foreign particles flying on the wind or sneakily catching air and water currents to high altitude rain forests, coral reefs or remote places of the Earth? Would they tell of these engineered materials being taken up by animals and sea creatures to lodge in fat cells or tissue and as a consequence, work up the food chain? These are the chemicals manufactured in a laboratory and never found in nature. They have been with us for a short time but evidently will remain as many that have been banned, such as DDT known to be a possible human carcinogen, are found in the environment and our bodies. The transgenerational impact is not known, nor is the ongoing effect of exposure at very low doses and in combination. Endocrine disrupting chemicals (EDC's) are a concern, especially in regard to new scientific thought that these may adversely interfere with the growing foetus when exposure happens at certain stages of development.

Examples of common EDC's, the products they can be found in and possible effects are:

Bisphenol A (BPA)

It is primarily used to make polycarbonate plastic and epoxy resins and found in countless products including toothbrushes, water bottles, dental sealants, paper money, receipts, CD's, children's toys, new cars, sporting equipment, medical supplies and epoxy-lined cans including those for soft drinks and infant formula. Elizabeth Grossman (2009, p 56) writes, "Rapidly accumulating scientific research indicates that bisphenol A is an endocrine disruptor and may be adversely affecting our ability to have children, our children's reproductive health, and even that of their children. Recent studies have also linked bisphenol A, which can mimic the hormone oestrogen, to obesity, breast and prostate cancer and to neurological problems." It is everywhere, used in the building and industrial industries, leaching into waterways and soils through waste disposal facilities and found in increasing levels in our oceans. High levels of this chemical have been found in adults, children and mothers' breast milk.

Parabens – (methyl paraben, propyl paraben, isobutyl paraben, ethyl paraben, butyl paraben, E216)

Parabens are used as preservatives and to increase the flexibility and softness in plastics. They are found in items such as personal care products including deodorants, shampoos, conditioners, shaving gel, toothpaste, hair spray, moisturisers, sunscreen, food and pharmaceuticals. Having oestrogen-like properties, they are linked to breast cancer and hormonal, reproductive and developmental defects in males and females.

Phthalates

Phthalates can be found in countless beauty products such as nail polish, body lotions, shampoos, deodorants, soaps, fragrances, cosmetics and household items such as air fresheners and cleaning substances. They are extensively used in the building industry, think PVC plastics used for vinyl flooring, and in the lining of food cans. Phthalates have been linked to endocrine disruption, birth defects, premature development, lowered sperm count, atherosclerosis, diabetes, allergies, asthma and are a suspected carcinogen. Being an oestrogen-like compound, they are linked to an increased breast cancer risk.

Chemicals that contaminate the air within our homes and buildings disrupt the finely tuned systems of the human body and are in almost everything we touch that is man-made; home appliances, furniture, carpets, electronics, toys, our toothbrush and those fashionable sunglasses. Non-stick coating on cookware can cause health problems due to the toxic gases, including known carcinogens, being released when high temperatures are reached. Natural materials used in clothing can be contaminated with dyes and chemicals during the manufacturing process. Toothpaste can contain toxic ingredients such as sodium lauryl sulphate, sorbitol, aspartame, fluoride and triclosan. I ask myself why a product designed to enter the mouth is labelled, 'Dangerous if swallowed' as it would be almost impossible for a small amount not to be swallowed and absorbed through the skin. Roach killers and stain repellants found in mattresses, including children's bedding, can release formaldehyde which is probably teratogenic (can interfere with foetal growth and cause birth defects) and is carcinogenic (cancer causing). Formaldehyde releasing ingredients are restricted or banned in countries such as Japan and the European Union.

Insect repellants can contain harmful chemicals such as DEET (N, N-diethyl-meta-toluamide) and permethrin. In 2002, Duke Today published the results of animal studies carried out by pharmacologist Mohamed Abou-donia, at the Duke University Medical Center, showing DEET to impair cell function in parts of the brain after prolonged use. Abou-donia said other potential side effects to humans include memory loss, headache, muscle weakness, fatigue and shortness of breath. He expressed concern for children due to subtle brain changes caused by chemicals in the environment, saying their skin more readily absorbs them and they potently affect developing nervous systems. Research is bringing to light the potential for transgenerational issues to occur. For example, scientists from the Washington State University published a study (Manikkam et al., 2012) in which pregnant rats were exposed to permethrin and DEET. The results showed the potential for the mother rats' great-granddaughters to have a higher risk of early puberty and malfunctioning ovaries with no exposure. "The take home message is to be safe and cautious when using insecticides," said Abou-donia. He cautions as to the use with children and when using with other insecticides and medications.

When a friend became ill with no apparent cause, it was concerning to learn that the culprit was chemical residue lingering in a lovely set of new sheets she snuggled into at night. This was discovered because her husband was a practitioner working with technology to detect environmental influences on our energetic system. Using the same technology, another lady's health was also restored. This time, the culprit was the sun streaming through a window and when heating a newly purchased cupboard, toxic chemicals from the timber leached into her underwear lying on the wooden shelving.

Toxic Metal Exposure

Cadmium, mercury, lead, arsenic and aluminium toxicity are avenues to explore not only when cancer is the issue but when early symptoms of disease present. Heavy metals, environmental toxins and pesticides, to name but a few, build up over the years and a combined overload can contribute to chronic illness. Blood tests can be carried out to determine the levels in the body. Toxicity can then be removed by a detoxification method called chelation therapy that can be given orally, intramuscularly or by administering an intravenous solution. Everyday detoxification methods include sweating, the regular use of infrared sauna therapy, enemas, Epsom salts baths, dry skin brushing and by adding herbs such as cilantro (coriander), chlorella and spirulina and dark green leafy plant food to your diet.

Cadmium, for example, is an endocrine disruptor and may increase the risk factor for endometriosis and conditions such as chronic fatigue, hypertension, osteoporosis, hypertension, depression, arthritis and migraines, to name but a few. It is found in food due to the use of bio-sludge fertilisers, a by-product of sewerage contaminated by toxic modern living, the burning of fossil fuels, incineration of plastics, galvanised pipes, batteries, amalgams, porcelain crowns and everyday household products. Waterways contaminated by industrial waste can contain cadmium.

I remember the conversation I had with my art teacher when his battle with prostate cancer was nearing an end and his revelation that he had been sent to Japan after the bombing to assist with the clean-up operations. Could the weakening from the ionising radiation he would have received at that time, combined with the continual use of chemicals in turpentine and toxic substances such as the lovely cadmium oranges, yellow and reds found in modern-day paints have contributed to his disease? Beatrice Hunter (2011, p 261) says cadmium barium red is highly toxic by chronic inhalation and ingestion. It may cause kidney damage, anaemia, the loss of ability to smell, gastrointestinal problems, damage to bone, teeth and liver and is a suspected human carcinogen associated with prostate and lung cancers. Orange and yellow cadmium pigments carry similar warnings. Sherry Rogers (2002, p 117) says, "It takes 20-50 years to stockpile enough to cause hypertension, osteoporosis, painful arthritis or to damage an organ or the mechanism for cholesterol control, or produce lung or prostate cancer, for example."

We Are Genetic Engineers

There are organic alternatives to personal hygiene products, household cleaners, children's toys, clothing, bed linen, household furniture and other items we use in our everyday lives. When having an awareness of the impact that environmental toxicity has on our health, we can make better choices. For instance, there are documented cases of children and teenagers diagnosed with asthma, attention-deficit hyperactivity disorder, oppositional defiant disorder and depression being restored to health when changes are made to the personal environment. Jean McDonald-Smith gives an example of this in her book, *How to Save the Planet from the Bathtub*. Her son's chemical sensitivities began during gestation but by changing his diet and using products containing safe ingredients, he is now problem free. She says how frightening it was to discover that everything we ingest and touch can have an effect on our unborn babies.

Programming for long-term mental and physical health issues begins before, during and after the gestation period. Stem cell biologist, Dr Bruce Lipton (2005, p 128) says, "Infants need a nurturing environment to activate the genes that develop healthy brains. Parents, the latest science reveals, continue to act as genetic engineers even after the birth of their child." Drs Wallach, Lan and Schrauzer (2014, p 362) confirm, "Preconception nurturing of one's body - both male and female, although the major responsibility is weighted towards the woman as embryonic success is dependent one hundred percent on the female's nutritional status - is essential to success and is a must if one is sexually active and still in the child-bearing years."

For many years, I have been aware of the dangers of chemicals taken into my body through the environment. It has been a slow process to change to environmentally friendly products but with a cancer diagnosis, I can no longer afford complacency. Unfortunately, it seems to be part of the human condition to almost have to experience a crisis to draw attention to what needs to be changed in our personal and worldly environments.

I discovered that since having chemotherapy, I have become more sensitive to chemicals. For instance, when strolling around the beautiful surrounds of a resort hotel after enjoying a delightful breakfast with friends, I became agitated and felt ill. Cleaners diligently wiping everything in sight with potent cleaning agents were found to be the culprits and when moving out of reach, I recovered. I am aware of the impact on my immune system of the never-ending assault from toxic substances and by lessening these in my personal environment, I know that my body will have the edge needed to heal.

CHAPTER 23

Nature's Pharmacy

A DAILY RECIPE FOR HEALING

A dose of sun and earth
Fresh air breathed into every cell in the body
Pure water empowered with words of grace
Organic, locally grown vegetables
A serving of fruit, nuts and berries
Ingested with prayers of gratitude
Greet the morning like a dear friend
Live each moment believing it to be a foundation for tomorrow
Delight in the sun's setting rays
Light a candle and say a blessing
When laying your head on a pillow at the day's end
Close your eyes and trust those dreams
For they will clear your mind and sooth torn emotions
Sleep will replenish every cell, tissue and organ
Your soul will sing a lullaby
While your heart beats a tune that is uniquely yours

(Ruchi Ananda, 2013)

Nature's Pharmacy Belongs to the People

It was once said to me that the best thing for a healthy life would be to have a personal chef to prepare food to nourish and replenish the body. One of life's joys is to share a home cooked meal with loved ones for this must surely nurture and replenish the heart. Growing food and sharing that bounty with neighbours or transforming it into a meal to nourish a family is an experience to feed the soul. Food is a part of the medicine story whether it is for healing the body, heart or soul.

Medicinal plants have always been used to maintain health. Handed down through the generations is information on how to make a tincture, poultice or tea to assist the healing process. Unfortunately, this time-trialled medical knowledge is little understood or valued in our modern Western culture where laws banning the practise of medicine by anyone not trained in a conventional medical school are enforced. However, today, there is an abundance of scientific research to support the healing properties of plants. Fingers are pointing to diet as the cornerstone for good health. Bodies need the correct input of fuel to function just as cars will only run when properly maintained. We are realising that popping a pill to regain lost health comes with a cost.

Wisdom teachings say for every illness there are plants growing nearby to assist the healing process. In the not too distant past, the herbalists of the day would wander hills, valleys and dales filling baskets with wild herbs needing no refrigeration, packaging and little processing. It has been said this may be the case if living in a rural area but when residing in a city consisting of housing complexes, concrete and little vegetation, this can no longer happen.

However, we can still grow edible plants in a kitchen garden or in pots on a verandah. It is said these will grow in alignment with our vibration and unlike putting together a concoction on an assembly line, the nourishment the plant produces will be uniquely for you. Sadly, this healing potential of fruit, vegetables and herbs is lost when toxic herbicides and pesticides replace the care and love needed by any plant to flourish. It is lost when the sacred DNA of the seed is violated with the insertion of a foreign gene causing a genome scrambling and a disorientation of its expression. It is lost when plants are nuked and transported around the world to be dosed with chemicals in order to maintain a healthy-looking appearance and when sprayed for mould whilst sitting on supermarket shelves.

It is important to purchase locally grown, in season produce and question whether this is so because the body needs the seasonal nutrients to align with the changing of the seasons. Even though produce may be organic, if it is grown out of season it may throw us out of balance. Winter is a time to go within, to be still in nature's dark womb to prepare for the coming of spring, a time to blossom and await the full flowering of potential during the summer period. Autumn brings the completion of a cycle, the sowing of a seed for a new beginning and a turning of the wheel of life. When eating in season and flowing with the cycles of nature we can lead healthy, peaceful lives.

The wisdom of the plant world is little understood today. It is said that a pet can assist the healing process and I believe plants can do the same. Research carried out by NASA and the Associated Landscape Contractors of America tells us that growing plants indoors can play a major role in assisting with the cleaning of our chemically polluted homes (Wolverton et al., 1989). The stories and legends associated with plants are soul enriching. My beautiful indoor lily, known to filter chemicals such as benzene, formaldehyde, ammonia, and trichloroethylene, is said to be associated with Mother Mary, given by the angel Gabriel when informing her of the destined birth of a child called Jesus. It is written in the *Second Book of Acts* (Guthrie, 1998, pp 18-19) that she planted it in the home of her mother, Anna. Here it bloomed once a month at the time of the new moon, withering before dawn at exactly the time Gabriel had come to her. She took it to her home at the passing of Anna where, instead of dying, it bore new shoots until her own passing surrounded by a garden of lilies, blooming for that grand occasion.

There are many traditional plant-based medical systems such as the Tibetan, American Indian, Amazonian, Australian aboriginal and Hawaiian. Today there is a renewed interest, one reason being the high cost of Western medication.

In China, Western medicine is used alongside Traditional Chinese

Medicine (TCM) and may include herbal medicine, acupuncture, massage and diet emphasising the quality (nutrient dense) and seasonal eating of food. In hospital pharmacies, seeds, twigs and the roots of plants are made into non-toxic remedies from formulas handed down through the generations. A patient in an oncology ward in China may be given these herbal remedies together with nutritional supplements and treatments such as chemotherapy.

Enjoying a revival in India is Ayurvedic medicine. It is a holistic approach, advocating preventative medicine and living in tune with nature to support physical, emotional and mental wellbeing. This ancient science dates back to the Vedic texts and is said to be perhaps the oldest documented natural healing system. However, just as doctors and scientists today can be prosecuted for practising holistic medicine, Ayurvedic colleges and clinics were banned when India was governed by Great Britain.

Bio-piracy also happens and for this reason codes for the names of plants when recording medical data was and is a widespread procedure. It is time to remember what indigenous cultures have always known, nature's pharmacy belongs to the people, not big corporations for profit and greed.

The Cancer Story and Diet

Many can testify to the healing benefits of changing to a healthy diet and lifestyle. However, when looking at the cancer story, we need to remember that everyone is different and it is wise to consult with your integrative practitioner, do your own research and listen to your body.

Dr Dean Ornish is an example of a doctor who is known for pioneering studies on lifestyle and disease. He is the founder and president of the Preventive Medicine Research Institute and the clinical professor at the University of California. Thirty-five years of research has led to published medical papers saying that a healthy diet and lifestyle can reverse heart disease and type II diabetes, turn on health-promoting genes and slow the aging process. He is currently carrying out research into slowing, stopping or reversing the progression of early-stage prostate cancer. The lifestyle medicine protocol he is using includes a whole-foods, plant-based diet, regular exercise (30 minutes walking, six days per week), stress reduction through yoga stretching and meditative practices and social support. Dr Ornish's work is funded by Medicare in the United States of America and more information can be found at www.ornishspectrum.com.

It was Dr William Koch, (1885-1967) professor of physiology at the Detroit Medical College, who researched and documented a process for curative success to be used in cancer therapy; detoxification, oxygenation and reconstruction. Using dietary means, the Gerson therapy, the Budwig diet and the Cilento Survival Plan are three examples that meet Dr Koch's criteria (Cilento 1993, p 187).

Dr Cilento's therapy is based on lifestyle changes, diet, raw juicing, relaxation techniques and supplements. Her book, *Heal Cancer*, gives this information.

A wealth of dietary information can be obtained from the books written by Max or Charlotte Gerson or visiting the Gerson Institute website where on-line workshops can assist in putting together a recovery plan. This diet requires that you have assistance in the preparation of juicing and food preparation. Not everyone has this kind of support as families lead busy lives. However, it is important for those supporting a loved one through the cancer maze to take an interest in the treatment plan and the chosen diet. Having someone to speak with who takes the time to understand and assist with the shopping, juicing and cooking can make a difference. Gentleness and kindness are keys that can open the door to wellness (also see Chapter 16).

Dr Johanna Budwig's cottage cheese, linseed formula, combined with healthy lifestyle changes has testimonials to success in helping to treat cancers such as breast, lung, brain, prostate, bone, carcinoma, bladder, cervical and stomach as well as leukaemia and Hodgkin's Disease. Cold-pressed, raw, unrefined, virgin linseed oil is the key as is the quality of the cottage cheese and the dietary food (also see Chapter 15).

People living in countries such as India, Japan, China and Southeast Asia have lower incidences of some cancers than those living in Western countries. A key is thought to be diet which consists largely of fruit, vegetables, herbs, spices and legumes. Professor Jane Plant used this knowledge and her scientific background to bring about a return to health from five recurrences of breast cancer that had spread to her lymph nodes. She noted that countries such as China and Japan had low breast and prostate cancer rates, but if people from these cultures adopted a western lifestyle, the rates increased accordingly. Professor Plant's personal diet was not so different in content to that eaten in these countries, however, with further investigation, discovered what she believed to be the missing link and that is dairy consumption.

Professor Plant attributes her healing and that of sixty-five other women, to the Plant Programme, outlined in her book, *Your Life in Your Hands*. This is a valuable source of information not only for breast and prostate cancer people but anyone seeking a cancer preventative lifestyle. By eliminating dairy products, Professor Plant (2000, p 125) says, "You will immediately and dramatically reduce the body's exposure to a powerful cocktail of hormones shown in experiment after experiment to promote breast and prostate cancer cell growth in cultures and/or experimental animals. You will also be reducing your exposure to antibiotic residues and other powerful biologically active chemicals, including man-made endocrine-disrupting chemicals, which can become particularly concentrated in milk."

The Mediterranean diet based on the consumption of vegetables, grains, fruits and fish with small amounts of poultry, eggs, yogurt and olive oil is known to lower the risk factor for diseases such as breast cancer, obesity and heart disease. The diet includes citrus fruit containing a powerful nutrient called d-limonene that has been shown to assist in the prevention of early stage carcinogenesis. The quality of the fruit is important as modern farming methods using chemical sprays and irradiation add an extra dose of toxins for the body to dispel. I was recently given a bag of freshly picked organic red grapefruit, known to have breast and prostate cancer fighting abilities. When grown in soil rich in nutrients such as lycopene and eaten close to harvesting, this fruit's promised bounty can be received.

Dr Sagen Ishizuka, born in 1851, was said to be the original founder of the Japanese macrobiotic medicine and diet that George Ohsawa evolved into the present-day macrobiotic diet. It was Dr Ishizuka's belief that sickness and physical weakness is caused by wrong eating habits (Aihara, 1986, p58). If he was speaking about the food of today, this would include canned, processed and fast foods containing additives, colourings, preservatives, processed sugar and hydrogenated vegetable oils. Included would be chemically laden dairy products, chicken and beef grown in factory farms, farmed fish and processed meats such as bacon, ham, sausages, corned beef and salami.

Dr Ishizuka's recipe for health would perhaps have consisted of eating a little wild fish, and food grown from nature's recipe in soil blessed with the sun's life-giving energy and watered with rain drops free from chemical residues. Today, this process is thwarted by poisons contaminating the air, water and earth and therefore, supplementation is often necessary for our bodies to obtain the fuel required to maintain health. It is important to be aware that the supplements we purchase from supermarkets and chemists may contain toxic fillers and synthetic ingredients. These add to the load our bodies purge on a daily basis and it is wise to source high quality products.

The story of how Dr Tatsuichiro Akizuki, the director of the Department of Internal Medicine at St. Francis Hospital in Nagasaki, protected his staff and patients from sickness after the terrible bombing in 1945 is well known. Dr Akizuki's success was attributed to a daily diet of miso soup garnished with wakame seaweed. It is known that many people included miso soup in their diet to assist in the prevention of radiation illness after the Chernobyl nuclear power plant accident in 1986.

The Nei Ching says, *"Even the highest medicine can cure only eight or nine out of ten sicknesses. The sicknesses that medicine cannot cure can be cured only by foods"* (Aihara, 1986, p 58).

BALANCE IS THE KEY

Western medicine has adopted a yang approach to healing. Cut, slash, burn, win the war on cancer and battle disease are thought forms instilled by governments, media advertising and a proportion of the present-day medical profession. The major turning point goes back to Louis Pasteur's (1822-1895) 'germ theory' saying that certain diseases are caused by the invasion of the body by organisms too small to be seen except through a microscope. Antoine Bechamp (1816-1908) was saying something different and saw microbes, bacteria, viruses and fungi as being everywhere including our bodies and not always the enemy but nature's way of moving sick and dead tissue. It is when the balance is upset from influences such as an acidic, low-oxygen environment caused by the ingestion of chemicals and impure water and food that the body's natural healthy state is compromised. Reid (1993, p 67) writes "Pasteur himself noted in his journals that each particular strain of bacteria he studies required a very specific and narrow range of temperature, moisture, light, pH balance, and other conditions in order to survive and multiply. If any of those conditions were altered or eliminated, the germ automatically perished." Another French scientist, Claude Bernard (1833-1878) agreed with Bechamp and it is told that Pasteur on his deathbed is reported to have said that Bernard was right, the microbe nothing and the environment everything. Could an overuse of today's antibacterial soaps, gels, lotions and potions designed to 'kill germs' be contributing to the opposite of the desired effect?

Many scientists are saying, "Yes."

We now understand that what we call our gut microbiome, a diverse mixture of microbes (including bacteria, funguses and viruses) that have evolved with us, play a vital role in maintaining physical, mental and emotional health. Nurturing this inner garden is key to maintaining balance. Imagine a scene in nature where the sky is blue, the air tingling with vitality, the sun is beaming rays of light onto a bubbling brook meandering through hills covered in wild flowers and herbs. Imagine this peaceful place after being desecrated by a bomb. The life-giving essence has now gone and nature's intricate balance is lost. This can be likened to our microbiome when it is bombarded with substances such as antibiotics, pesticides, herbicides, toxic chemicals and genetically modified food. When the food we eat, the water we drink, the air we breathe and the earth we walk on saturate our bodies with man-made chemicals, how can we not become ill? Many are not aware that these factors may be contributing to an internally desecrated environment where pathogenic microbes flourish, causing imbalance and disease to occur. However, the opposite occurs when we fertilise our internal garden with high quality food (organic, locally grown and in season if possible) and pure water. Sleep, meditation, gentle exercise such as yoga and deep breathing, spending time in a natural environment and positive emotions such as love, compassion, joy and peace, nourish the gut flora. Healing and nurturing foods such as slow cooked bone broth and fermented vegetables frequented our table when I was a child and today, are experiencing a return to grace. These foods soothe achy joints, pacify the adrenals and bring healing to the gut eco system.

It was Walter Cannon (1871-1945), a physiologist, who realised the significance of balance, or homeostasis, within the many body fluids with differing pH factors. An example is the importance of maintaining a slightly alkaline blood pH level at 7.4. A slightly alkaline body fluid sustains life whereas the cumulative effect of acidic body fluids is a major contributory factor to creating disease. This happens when consuming toxic substances that change the environment in which our cells can happily, live and thrive. Herman Aihara (1986, p 9) said, "Cancer is a condition in which body cells become abnormal due to the abnormal condition of body fluids." Cancer cells love to splash in acidic puddles.

Litmus paper designed to test urine or saliva and a naturopathic practitioner to prescribe supplementation to assist in correcting an imbalance is valuable. Having knowledge of alkaline and acid forming foods is important. Most fruit and vegetables are considered to be alkaline forming foods as it is the condition foods create in the body after being eaten that is the key. For example, when I squeeze a fresh lemon into a glass of filtered water each morning, the acidic elements in the fruit when oxidised in the body become alkaline, neutralising body acid. This can be a powerful way to rehydrate offering health benefits such as assisting to flush the nightly build-up of toxins from the body.

Processed, genetically modified food, meat and dairy containing antibiotics and hormones contribute towards tipping the balance to acidity. I believe that making small changes in diet and lifestyle can make a difference. For instance, I learnt when visiting the nature farms in Japan (see World of Beauty) that it takes three days for our taste buds to return to normal when eating organic food. This concept applies to our whole body. After a time of eating healthy, the body will become more in tune with its needs allowing ancestral wisdom residing in cells to be heard through those gut promptings. Keeping the bodily processes in correct balance to maintain health is the job of the innate wisdom of our body. It is our job to support this finely tuned process by having an awareness of diet, lifestyle choices and the importance of mental, emotional and spiritual wellbeing. Seeking the support of an integrative professional is important as blood type, lifestyle, personal medical history and medications to name but a few factors come together to make a unique person.

CANCER FIGHTING FOOD

Cancerous lumps and bumps can be removed, but circulating tumour cells resistant to radiation treatment and chemotherapy can spread to vulnerable parts of the body and morph into another tumour. This is why it is important to have an integrative practitioner on your team who has knowledge of the plant kingdom's ability to assist in the removal of cancer cells while leaving healthy cells untouched. Scientists are verifying what our ancestors knew; nature's pharmacy has a safe and effective answer to our ills. An example being a published paper by Scarpa and Ninfali (2015) reviewing thirty years of research on the ability of phytochemicals and herbal extracts to induce apoptosis (cancer cell death) without harming healthy cells. These include: polyphenol epigallocatechin-3-gallate (green tea), curcumin (turmeric), resveratrol (grapes), lycopene (tomatoes), luteolin (cabbage, spinach), genistein (fermented soy), oleanolic acid (extra virgin olive oil), beta-carotene (carrots) and sulforaphane (the cruciferous family).

However, we must play our part. I add kale leaves and other members of the cruciferous or brassica vegetable group to my daily green juice whenever possible as these have cancer preventative and fighting abilities, as shown in the above-mentioned research. Kale, for example, is high in carotenoids, vitamin C, calcium and boasts a healthy omega-3 to omega-6 ratio, to name but a few health-giving benefits. Like most vegetables, kale is alkalising and assists with maintaining the pH balance. Broccoli sprouts contain glucoraphanin, the precursor to sulforaphane that plays a role in turning on protective genes in the body and turning off cancer promoting genes. Other members of this vegetable family include broccoli, cauliflower, Brussels sprouts, cabbage, radish, turnips, bok choy, kohlrabi, mustard and collard greens and mizuna. These are nutrient dense and boast scientifically proven health benefits.

Studies show the effectiveness of the allium vegetable family including shallots, leeks, chives and garlic in assisting to prevent disease. Garlic, for instance, has potent cancer fighting properties and like all vegetables in this and the cruciferous group, leaves normal cells intact. Garlic possesses antibiotic, antiviral, antifungal and antimicrobial properties. It plays a part in preventing and treating infections, DNA damage, mercury poisoning and can assist in reducing the effects of radiotherapy. In ancient times, garlic was considered to have magical properties that could protect against the forces of black magic, vampires and the plague. It is written in cultural folk-lore, such as the Chinese and Greek traditions, that if a clove of garlic is given to a newborn by a grandmother, it will protect against the evil eye.

Friends came to visit with a box of ginger chocolate, a gift saying they remember the little things I love, such as the pretend squabbles over the ginger jam. It is comforting to have friends who shared those vulnerable teenage years and stayed to witness the ups and downs of life's journey. It has all come and gone, but not the friendship spanning almost a lifetime, represented by a box of ginger chocolate. Ginger is a recognised medicinal plant used to treat colds, nausea, fever, tetanus, leprosy and arthritis, to list but a few benefits. It was called, 'the universal medicine' in India. Scientific research has verified over one hundred medicinal uses including pain relief, morning sickness, flatulence, heart health and it has been shown to have cancer preventative and treatment abilities. For more information see: www.greenmedinfo.com.

My mother insists on having her main meal in the middle of the day, the evening meal usually consisting of bananas. At the time of writing, she is ninety-four years old, escapes under the doctor radar, taking no pills or potions, her only complaint being rickety joints and bones. When doing a little research, we are now not concerned about her eating habits as it has long been known that a heavy meal taken prior to bedtime is not wise. The body utilises little calories when asleep and taking excess food at this time can generate free radical damage contributing to chronic disease and the aging process. Bananas are rich in pectin, iron, vitamins, potassium and magnesium needed to build enzymes that play a vital role in every bodily process. Enzymes, however, are not found in cooked or processed food and as the Western diet can open the way to a deficiency, supplementation may be necessary.

Raw vegetable juicing can be an excellent way to take in nourishment when loss of appetite is an issue. By adding carrot juice to my daily regime, the body is given the cancer fighting beta-carotene in an easily digested form. Apple juice gives many health benefits including the ability to assist in removing heavy metals such as cadmium and lead from the body. Raw beetroot juice boasts health benefits such as dissolving stones in the liver, kidneys and bladder to being a blood purifier. In the 1950's, the Hungarian physician, Dr Alexander Ferenczi discovered the tumour-inhibiting effect of the flavonoid betazyane that is found in beets. He clinically recorded success in treating cancer with raw beetroot juice. When freshly made from living foods, juices are an excellent way to flood the body with the nutrients needed to repair and heal after an illness or toxic treatments. Other benefits include detoxifying the body and the maintenance of health.

Perhaps our body's cries for the nutrients it needs is a contributory factor to the present-day addiction crises. Charlotte Gerson and Beata Bishop (2010, p 87) believe this to be true and say, "Apart from all other factors, most addictions are caused - or at least aggravated - by nutritional deficiency." They point out that a patient's cravings and withdrawals can be alleviated by an hourly dose of freshly pressed organic juice.

HEALING HERBS

Herbal teas can be a valuable addition to diet but can come packaged in little bags containing chemicals that do not belong in a medicinal brew. Therefore, sourcing the purest form possible is advisable. To enhance the powerful healing effects of water and herb, create your own 'tea ceremony' by bringing mindfulness and gratitude to the process of preparing and serving.

There are numerous herbal teas to source or consult with your natural practitioner and some well-known ones are horsetail, calendula, pawpaw leaf and green tea. Along with a semi-vegetarian diet, fenugreek is believed by folk healers around the world to assist in the healing of breast tumours. Chamomile, thyme, peppermint, lemon balm teas and dandelion root coffee, contain a substance called apigenin that plays a role in apoptosis, a process supporting cancer cells to die after a time instead of growing stronger. Apigenin is found in vegetables and fruit, such as parsley, celery, garlic, onions, oranges and bell pepper. Many herbs are known to have cancer preventative and fighting qualities, some being aloe vera, angelica root, astragalus, burdock root, chlorella, ginseng, licorice root and cat's claw. Dose and quality are important as is taking into consideration the type of cancer and seeking the advice of a practitioner trained in herbal medicine when dealing with chronic illness.

The Mulberry Tree

I remember treading along bush tracks on my way home from school, picking a bunch of jonquils, daises and daffodils growing wild but sadly, by the time I had entered high school this beautiful terrain had gone. The rocky road in front of our home, the dirt footpath on which we rode our homemade billycarts and the acres of surrounding market gardens had disappeared. Industrialisation was seeping into the suburban landscape and concrete footpaths and roads were replacing nature's countryside. In my imagination, however, I can still revisit the former rich landscape to make a wish by blowing the seeds off the stem of a dandelion and I now know that what I thought to be a weed, has remarkable healing qualities. Conditions such as gout, anaemia, arthritis, liver, pancreas, bladder and kidney problems have been found to benefit. In combination with other herbs, it has been used in Traditional Chinese Medicine (TCM) for the treatment of breast, lung and uterine tumours and due to its diuretic properties, has been found to assist with fluid retention during chemotherapy. Research carried out in 2015 by Siyaram Pandey, a senior biochemist at the University of Windsor, has received funding for a clinical trial to begin on the anti-cancer potential of dandelion root extract. His laboratory successfully demonstrated the herb's ability to induce apoptosis in human melanoma cells without destroying healthy cells.

What will we say when the children of the future ask, "Where have the wild herbs gone?"

Wild plants hold the highest vibration. They grow to the orchestrated genius of mother nature by drawing in the essence of fire, earth, air and water to produce a vitamin 'pill' filled with wild energy. Indigenous peoples lived by this sacred knowledge but it was suppressed when European settlers colonised these cultures. For instance, the Australian aborigines, the country's first people whose roots are said to date back to over forty thousand years, had sophisticated knowledge of the cultivation and application of native plants. Although awareness of this sacred knowledge has dimmed, there is a revived interest today. However, we need to ask, "Will herbal medicine be valued as a healing modality alongside conventional treatment?" Safe and effective herbal remedies have been banned in favour of harsh chemicals, the main reason being, financial profit. Pharmaceutical companies also artificially synthesise and imitate herbal plants so they can be patented, an example being aspirin. The active ingredient found in aspirin is salicylic acid also found in the bark of the white willow tree, used in natural medicine to treat headaches.

Wild crafted plants are threatened by modern-day living such as the destruction of rain forests, polluted marine environments, development of large city conglomerates and the spraying of toxic chemicals. I remember the day I was driving along our hinterland road to be greeted by a counsel truck spraying the roadside vegetation. Although the windows in the car were up, it took hours to recover from the dose of poison experienced on that beautiful day. I cringe when I see men in bright coloured garments spraying parks, playgrounds and sporting fields with chemicals that science is now saying are far from safe. These are the areas where children experience a connection with nature and it is sad to think that health and environmental issues for generations to come may be the result.

Naturopath, Dorothy Hall in her 1976 classic, *The Natural Health Book* suggests we take a second look at weeds and wild plants not only for the incredible survival instincts they possess but also the healing benefits. For instance, she says the wild strawberry has five times the dietary value of its 'better bred cousin'. A lady I knew worked on a strawberry farm and was forced to leave because of health problems attributable to the chemicals used in growing one of our most precious fruit. Non-organic strawberries made it to the top of the Dirty Dozen list published by the Environmental Working Group (EWG) in 2016. Some of the chemicals used on this fruit have been linked to cancer and reproductive, hormonal and neurological problems (www.ewg.org/foodnews). When organically grown, strawberries, rich in essential nutrients and phytochemicals, can assist in nullifying the effects of alcohol consumption. Nature's Pharmacy contains plants that have value in counteracting the effects of toxic chemicals and heavy metals. Mother Nature has been in the manufacturing business far longer than man has walked upon the Earth and her safety record is without blemish. During our short visit to her realm, all she asks is that we tread softly with gratitude in our hearts for the bounty and beauty she bestows.

The wild energy from wild plants such as the mulberry fruit known to grow in any climate on Earth is soul food, supporting our human DNA. The mulberry fruit and leaf can be found in the traditional medicine of cultures such as Japan, China, Asia and India. I have childhood memories of the mulberry tree we had at the foot of our garden. It provided delicious fruit and Poppy rolled flour into pastry to make pies served with a special treat, a dollop of cream. It gave us silk worm cocoons that we spun into bookmarks. Birds rested in its branches chirping songs of the tree's stoic history. What delightful gifts the old tree gave and I often wonder whether our technological world of today has robbed children of this experience. Where are the mulberry trees, those wise ancient guardians of a past now growing dim? Will children ever again climb your trunk, eat your fruit and spin your yarn or will they only know a world of plastic shelter, food and toys? Will they hear your whispered teachings?

Ancient physicians knew that wild mushrooms had healing properties to support the maintenance of health and the prevention of disease. It is believed that over fifty mushrooms existing today have anti-carcinogenic effects. These include the Chinese cordyceps and the Japanese enoki, reishi, karawatake, maitake and shitake. I remember the Sunday drive to a country area and picking wild mushrooms under the friendly gaze of a farmer who was pleased to be sharing his bounty. I remember picking wild blackberries growing alongside roads seeing little traffic and Poppy baking pies to serve with that dollop of cream. Bags were filled with manure to feed our small garden consisting of lettuce, tomatoes and spinach, to name but a few.

We were never really ill, just the odd sniffle or childhood infection such as measles, mumps or chicken pox. No-one I knew suffered ill effects, being nurtured by wise parents who knew this to be nature's way of triggering young immune systems to become strong in order to sustain a lifetime of living. Anthroposophical wisdom says childhood infections can be an important process in a child's development, assisting inherited tendencies to be released to support the child to make the body a more comfortable home. I have heard it said that the generations of children we are seeing now have weakened immune systems, attributable in part to receiving copious vaccinations before the immune function is fully developed. There is strong evidence to suggest that vaccinations when given in combination, increase the risk of side effects occurring. Has the most important system we have for fighting disease, one that has remained strong throughout eons of time, grown weak in its efforts to fight cancer cells roaming the body?

When a babe in arms, Cleveland's reaction to the whooping cough vaccine was frightening; he nearly lost his life suffering a febrile convulsion and developed whooping cough which doctors refused to acknowledge. It was a nursing sister who heard that awful cough and said, "That child has whooping cough." Looking back, I wonder as to the vague symptoms he experienced during the first seven years of his life that doctors said were in my mind. At the time, I travelled a long distance to see the doctor

I grew up with whose belief it was that a mother is the one to listen to when it comes to her child. He also gave me a healthy respect for the modern wonder drugs, rarely prescribing them if a natural medicine could be used.

When Cleveland stopped breathing on that terrible night, I bundled him into the car with a nanna in tow, glamorous in bare feet and skimpy night attire. We were received at a local doctor's surgery with rude hostility, even though there was after-hours availability. The public hospital being miles away in a nearby town, we made a frantic dash to a private facility. The care Cleveland received that night and over the next day or so may have saved his life and the doctor was asked to apologise. Later that night, I realised I had driven the car with no glasses. I am extremely short-sighted and have heard an eye doctor comment, "Never let that woman behind a wheel without glasses!" Oh, the wonder of motherhood!

Cancer was not heard of in the young when I was growing up. We were standing on the brink of a new era in environmental changes contributing to high risk factors in children due to their size and developmental process. Like those school children in Japan who were given a daily lunch from the MOA nature farms (see World of Beauty) we ate organic vegetables and fruit on a daily basis. We played outside in the fresh air, free to visit neighbouring friends, explore and climb that mulberry tree.

Where are the mulberry trees, wild blackberry bushes and fields of mushrooms? I am grateful to have memories of those jaunts to country areas, backyards filled with vegetable gardens and that wise overseer, the mulberry tree. I am grateful to have friends who hop on an aeroplane to bring me a box of ginger chocolates. I am grateful I had a wise doctor who practised integrative medicine. Perhaps because of this, my life today has been prolonged with quality time as I had the knowing to seek practitioners with a similar wisdom and knowledge.

Chapter 24

The Web of Life

"Spider Woman is our link to the past and the future
Weaving our dreams into our destiny
Her threads link to the heavens and the underworlds
She is the weaver of the web of life."

(Ruchi Ananda, 2013)

Tears gushed from the cherry blossom trees on that terrible day in 1945 when Japan was nuked using nuclear warfare. When Japan was nuked again in 2011 and deadly radioactive elements spewed from the Fukushima nuclear plant to make their way around the world, the cherished plant life wept. Many have died and will die, become deformed and ill because of this day, one that had its seeding with the dropping of the bombs on Hiroshima and Nagasaki.

Are we a lost people without a connection to the web of life, now tarnished, torn and in tatters? How do we reconnect the broken cords and disconnect from the illusion we call modern society? One fed to us through newspapers, television, religions, politicians and the gods and goddesses of the day such as sporting heroes, actors, actresses and icons of the music world whose glamour promises that it too could be ours. However, those with dark eyes and protruding bones seen on the front pages of magazines more often than not disappear through a revolving door leading to a rehabilitation centre. Reading tales of their woeful journeys has become food and nourishment for our minds.

The real news happening in our world is rarely reported in glossy magazines, nor is it told in news broadcasts flashed relentlessly into our subconscious minds. We are not told that the Fukashima contamination of the water we drink, the air we breathe and the food we eat is continuing on a daily basis. Dumped into the Pacific Ocean are vast amounts of carcinogenic radioactive isotopes such as strontium-90 which can mimic the properties of calcium, concentrate in the breasts of lactating women and years later lead to breast cancer. Babies drinking contaminated cow, goat or human milk are exposed to a future possibility of cancer of the bone or leukaemia. Frank Walker (2014, p 193) tells us that a major scientific anti-bomb conference held in Pugwahs, Canada in 1957, advised that strontium-90 from nuclear fallout could irreversibly harm the human race.

We do not hear Dr Leuren Moret, an internationally recognised geoscientist and specialist on the environmental and biological effects of ionising radiation, say that the bomb testing in the early 1960's altered the DNA of people worldwide; there is no safe dose of radiation, the effects are cumulative and an offspring who inherits a parent's history of radiation in genes, passed on through the sperm or egg, is already weakened. Dr Moret speaks of serious health situations that can arise with further exposure due to disasters such as Fukushima, eating the resultant contaminated dairy or sea food, frequent flying through Fukushima fallout, medical and dental ex-rays and airport scanning equipment. Therefore, with a build-up of radiation of which the person may be completely unaware, a small dose can trigger a health crisis such as brain, thyroid, neuromuscular and lymphatic system damage, seizures or hair loss. Flu-like symptoms are a common short-term effect and leukaemia, lymphoma or cancer can be a long-term consequence (Consolo, 2013).

In his book, *Maralinga*, journalist and author, Frank Walker, gives a chilling account of how the long and short-term consequences of the 1950's atomic bomb testing carried out by the British in the Australian outback were covered up. The impact on the lives of military personnel involved in these operations has never been acknowledged, nor have the ongoing health issues affecting the lives of their children and grandchildren. The extent of fallout on the general population was not revealed. Radioactive particles can concentrate in food chains resulting in future genetic disease, leukaemia and cancer. We need to ask what part those tests played in the cancer epidemic we are experiencing today. The extent of veteran early death and homelessness, due to physical and mental illness resulting from exposure to radioactive pollution caused by military activities, to this day remains cloaked in secrecy.

Unless we listen to Dr Helen Caldicott, a leading voice in the anti-nuclear movement warning of the consequences of the medical hazards of the nuclear age, we will not feel the tears in her words when she tells us the United States used uranium in Fallujah and Baghdad, Iraq. As a consequence, Dr Caldicott says that in Fallujah, eighty percent of the babies born are grossly deformed and leading doctors tell women to stop having babies. Regarding the nuclear age, "This is the greatest public health hazard the world has ever witnessed, apart from the threat, every day, of nuclear war," she said (Heyes, 2011).

We cannot escape radiation exposure as it comes from natural causes such as radon gases, decay of radium in the earth, thorium and potassium found in the earth's crust, the sun and space. This has always been the case, but today exposure from man-induced radiation greatly compounds the problem. Pregnant women, children and people with gene mutations whose bodies are less able to repair damage to their DNA are most at risk. At the time of writing, an estimated one in two Australian men and one in three women are expected to experience cancer before the age of eighty-five, suggesting that causes need to be addressed rather than optimistically hoping for the magic pill.

Japanese farmers say the ties between the soil, the people and the web of life were disabled on that fateful day in 2011. The farmers, however, are continuing to sow despite an uncertain future amid enormous contamination that can remain for tens of thousands of years. Their words saying that this is all the more reason to seek the way to an organic future, need to be heard (IFOF, 2012).

CHAPTER 25

Water

———— ⟲ ————

"Quality and purity of our drinking water is one
of the most important health choices a person can make."

(David Perlmutter, 2017)

Dr Henri Coanda, a Romanian Nobel Prize Winner, spent many
years studying water and its buffeting effects against disease. He
found that people residing in unpolluted areas such as the Hunza Valley
often lived to a healthy, happy, one hundred plus years. The water they
drank was thought to be a major factor, along with a clean organic diet.
Water tested in the Hunza Valley was shown to have a high alkaline pH
and a high level of active hydrogen and colloidal mineral content. This is
living water that may have fallen eons ago to form glacial mountains and
to one-day flow into the valley below, the water our bodies dream about
when living in polluted cities. As all water is connected and has memory
and we are approximately seventy percent water, perhaps disease is a
striving to return to this pristine state as nature intended.

We are energy vibrating at a certain frequency. Whatever we take into
ourselves by sight, smell, touch, word, thought or ingestion affects our
vibration and whatever we give from ourselves, influences the vibration
of our environment. Each subatomic part resonates to a vibration and
our mind and body are influenced accordingly. When I became ill some
years ago, the practitioner I was seeing at the time used technology to

measure the vibrations of the organs of the body. Some were found to be resonating so low that it was a wonder I could walk and talk. He corrected the imbalances by using the same technology to transfer the essence of what was needed to do this into a small bottle of water (shown scientifically to be a carrier of information). When ingested, this information was relayed to the subatomic particles of the body to correct the disturbed vibration. This is how homeopathic remedies work and why they are successful.

The drugs used by Western medicine work on the cellular level where symptoms appear, however, imbalances usually originate at the subatomic level. Suppressing symptoms can work for a time but the body will always strive for balance. The out of balance distortion will eventually show itself, possibly in other symptoms in another part of the body, just as water will always find its own level.

The late Dr Fereydoon Batmanghelidj (2008) agreed that water has life-giving and life-sustaining properties. He believed that the lack of water or dehydration is the primary cause of disease states and can play a major part in the onset of migraine headaches and an underlying role in many diseases such as arthritis, depression, chronic fatigue syndrome and hypertension. Indeed, we are aware that the morning after a night on the town can become less traumatic when drinking water before going to bed.

Could it be true that by drinking ample water, some of our health issues can be eliminated? Dr Batmanghelidj said, "Yes," but, what if the water we drink contains a cocktail of poisons such as lead, aluminium, mercury, cadmium, asbestos, pesticides, pharmaceuticals, chlorine and fluoride?

Fluoride

Toxins from our consumer-based lifestyle are now found in unacceptable levels, not only in our bodies, but also our water supplies and some, such as fluoride, are put into public water systems by governments. This may open the proverbial can of worms but there is scientific evidence to say that fluoride is a toxic industrial waste byproduct. The evidence is weak when looking at the tooth decay argument.

When speaking of the ethical argument, Drs Connett, Beck and Micklem (2010, pp 5, 31) state: "Because there are so many unanswered health questions, fluoridation of water must be considered an ongoing experimental procedure, and as such it is a violation of the Nuremberg Code, which forbids experimentation on humans without their informed consent." They write that governments of fluoridated countries have made little effort to study the results of animal studies linking fluoride and disease. Fluoride is linked to increased bone fractures in children, arthritic-like symptoms in adults, lowered IQ in children, the accumulation of fluoride in the pineal gland, the lowering of melatonin production and the early onset of puberty. According to William Fischer (2000, p 246), laboratory studies show that low doses of fluoridated water can cause serious genetic and chromosomal damage to plants, animals and humans.

Fluoride's ability to displace iodine is another concern as iodine is needed by every cell in our body for optimum health and plays a crucial role in breast health. Journalist and researcher, Lynne Farrow (2013, p 52) says, "In animals, blocking dietary iodine will cause the breasts to swell, develop nodules, fibrous tissue and cysts in a way that parallels the progressive development of breast disease in women. When iodine is supplied, the fibrocystic disease goes away. When iodine is blocked again, the breast disease returns." Ms Farrow is not alone in believing that iodine deficiency has become a health crisis. Having your iodine levels checked by an integrative practitioner and eliminating iodine-blocking toxins are important steps to consider when breast cancer is the issue.

Dr Bruce Spittle (2008, pp 2-3) says that fluoride fatigue (not relieved by sleep) is an illness that is not officially recognised and is a part of the fluoride story. He outlines a long list of clinical symptoms that may signal fluoride toxicity in humans, including chronic fatigue, headaches, muscular weakness, skin rash or itching, especially after showering or bathing, mouth sores (also occurring with the use of fluoridated toothpaste), depression, nervousness and dizziness. He cites the work of Dr Susheela who is the executive director of the Fluorosis Research and Rural Development Foundation in Delhi, India. Dr Susheela made a similar list and stated that fluoride toxicity should also be suspected when repeated miscarriages, still births, male infertility and dental fluorosis are a problem.

European populations as well as countries such as China, India and Japan drink non-fluoridated water (Connett, Beck and Micklem 2010, p 31). Fluoride is a recognised drug that has not undergone adequate testing. The recommended dose is much lower than what would be consumed by people taking in a combination of tap water, manufactured drinks, processed food where fluoridated water is used and foods grown with fertilisers containing fluorides. This is not to mention the absorption through the skin when bathing and showering, from toothpaste, dental restorations and medications. What is an unapproved drug linked to a long list of suspected health risks doing in our drinking water?

Purifying Water

It is wise to install a filter as it is pointless eating chemical free food and then giving our bodies a large dose of chemicals from another source to deal with on a regular basis. Bottled water is a concern and testing has shown some to contain contaminants or be filtered tap water that has never seen that crystal spring advertised on the bottle. Plastic bottles are another concern. It is wise to use stainless steel water containers, especially when travelling to avoid the heating of plastic which may cause the leaching of toxic chemicals. If you buy bottled water it is important to ensure that it is not exposed to heat or sunlight.

Dr Masaru Emoto (2003), a Japanese researcher, discovered that by flash freezing water after it had received a positive thought or a written or spoken word, it formed beautiful hexagonal crystals. When a negative word was thought, written or spoken before flash freezing, the result resembled a malformed pool of dirty water. Tap water containing chemicals revealed a horrible structure lacking life force but as Dr Emoto's work revealed, words are reflected in water that can be changed by intention, beautiful music and high vibrational thought or word. Many cultures use this science such as the American Indians and the

Jewish people; the use of holy water in rituals such as baptism is an example.

We cannot migrate to a remote unpolluted place where water flows naturally over rocky terrain creating a health and life-giving elixir. However, as Dr Emoto has shown, we can restructure water to align with its true nature and become a healthier less polluted substance. This can be done in many ways and examples are as follows:

- Fill dark blue glass bottles or wrap dark blue cellophane around glass containers without the lids. Leave in the sun for at least three hours. The colour blue will help to transmute toxins such as chlorine and fluoride.
- It is wise to source the best water or filter to suite your daily use. A high-quality carbon filter portable system can be used when travelling. Attach a copy of Dr Emoto's beautiful water crystals, formed after hearing the words "I love you" or "Thank you".
- Enclose a glass of filtered water with your hands and make the intention that everything you need for healing will be transmuted into the water. Imagine these qualities flowing through the crown of your head into the heart centre and out through your hands into the glass. Give gratitude, "I love you and I thank you," before drinking the water and know that it is blessing every cell in your body.
- Dr Cousens (2014) says, "Based on the ancient Kabalistic understanding that water is One world soul, whenever we bless our water in a conscious heartfelt way, we send out messages of peace, Love, gratitude and we are linked to the cellular water in all people and in Nature. As we resonate with our mature water we resonate with water everywhere and in that process, resonate with all souls and the very soul of the planet."

THE ETHERIC BODY

It is important to health and wellbeing to have an understanding of what Rudolf Steiner called the etheric or life body which is a template of the physical but existing on a subtler vibration. Carried via blood, lymph and cellular fluids to interpenetrate the physical body, it is during the first seven years of life that the etheric helps grow the physical and the nervous system. Thereafter, it plays a major role in building, maintaining, protecting and ensuring health. To support this process, creative activities such as painting, singing, playing in the mud, climbing trees and storytelling are important. Bryant (1993, p 61) states, "Educators and parents too easily forget that the early childhood is built from feelings, imagination, fantasy, and dreams." He suggests that our obsession today with the mind and the push for early intellectual maturity undermines the physical and emotional development and freezes creativity. Anthroposophical teachings say that too much intellectual activity given during these early years can weaken the physical body, contributing to degenerative disease and premature aging in later life. As with all developmental stages, it is not just the physical body in the process of becoming, it is our whole being and during these delicate formative years a child is vulnerable. If the experience is not one of nurture, love and safety, then the incarnation process may not flow as intended, resulting in emotional and physical illnesses in later life.

Having an awareness of the interaction of the etheric field with the physical body plays a part in understanding cancer. From an anthroposophical point of view, illness in any area of the body indicates a local breakdown in the etheric body. Dr Michael Evans and Iain Rodger (2000, p 25) say, "This breakdown allows the cells to reproduce in an uncontrolled way and ultimately to damage the rest of the organism. Therefore, a more appropriate therapy for cancer would be one which helped to restore the formative forces in the area where the cancer had arisen."

Depletion can occur through stress, man-made chemicals, radiation, electromagnetic frequencies and lack of contact with the four elements, especially pure water as the etheric closely relates to water. Rhythm, balance, relaxation, interaction with nature and those who offer warmth, love and nurturing are food for the etheric body. It is when the physical and the etheric are in alignment that we can experience a wonderful feeling of inner peace and practices such as pranayama, acupuncture, yoga, Tai Chi, Qigong and Reiki can assist in bringing about this balance. Another example is Paneurhythmy, an ancient and sacred dance that can take the body to flow with the forces of nature.

Unlike living food and water from nature's womb, conventionally grown food and tap water with added chemicals have little or no etheric field. We need living sustenance to remain vibrant beings as this is what the etheric uses when weaving a physical body and patching and mending one that is broken. One of our greatest challenges today is to maintain that level of aliveness despite the ways of modern society.

From the beginning of my cancer journey, I have taken a supplement to support my body to achieve the required alkalinity to maintain wellness, that is until discovering a spring water source. Within weeks of drinking this living water I began testing a perfect alkalinity and experiencing an increased overall wellness. Over time, I have been detoxifying and cleansing body cells, however, I do believe the water (bottled from the ground the day before purchase) dancing with the essence of life has made a difference and recent blood tests say this is the case.

Perhaps water is a messenger of hope telling us we can bring alignment to our being by changing the way we live. It is up to us whether we become muddy puddles or beautiful crystals reflecting life.

CHAPTER 26

World of Beauty

*"In human beings, it is the beauty of the
mind - that is, beauty of the spirit.
Of course, there must also be beauty of words
and conduct. This is individual beauty.
The expansion of individual beauty produces social beauty."*

(Mokichi Okada, 2005)

As a child, I delighted in playing in the dirt, adding water and seeing the transformation into puddles of mud. Our back yard grew an abundance of fresh vegetables and chickens and ducks were free to scratch and peck. My favourite was a chook called Daisey who loved to be dressed in a frilly gown and bonnet and pushed around in the doll's pram. Touching the earth, breathing uncontaminated air, soaking in the life-giving rays from the sun and eating fresh organic vegetables surrounded by animals that were a part of our family, was the perfect blueprint for growing bodies. Every meal was blessed, "Thank you for the world so sweet, thank you for the food we eat, thank you for the birds that sing, thank you God for everything." Looking back, I enjoyed abundant health and appreciate my parents for giving me this foundation.

In the year 2008, I visited Japan and spent three days at MOA International witnessing a similar concept on a much larger scale. I have included this part of my Japan journey as I believe that it will uplift your spirits to read about what could be a blueprint for creating a new world. Change begins with us and by creating our own personal World of Beauty, we bring beauty to the whole, ensuring the inheritance we leave is a world our grandchildren will feel blessed to inherit.

MY INTRODUCTION TO MOA INTERNATIONAL

I arrived at Atami station to be greeted by a placard bearing my name, held by Tak who was to guide me through the concept of Mokichi Okada's World of Beauty.

MOA International is the work of Mokichi Okada, born in Tokyo in 1882, he passed over in 1955. Being a scientist of the future who foresaw the troubled times of today, Mr Okada envisioned the creation of a civilised world in which spiritualism and materialism as well as Eastern and Western civilisations would live in harmony. Seeing the possibility of a world where all lives would be filled with radiance, he set about establishing organisations for the purpose of researching his concepts and achieving his philosophical ideas. He called this a 'World of Beauty'.

In the period following World War II, Mr Okada collected works of art to prevent these from being sold overseas and established the Tomei Art Presentation Society. In 1982, the centennial year of his birth, the MOA Museum of Art opened in Atami. My personal introduction was the sculpture of *King and Queen* by Henry Moore, overseeing a wondrous ocean outlook and sandstone steps leading into the main building. On the journey to the main lobby, I felt like I was riding to heaven on two hundred meters of escalators, gliding through domed-shaped, soft-pastel changing colour. At this time, the museum held approximately three thousand, five hundred works of art including three National Treasure pieces and sixty-five Cultural Property items. It boasts a theatre offering seasonal performances and a Golden Tea Room. The first works of art I encountered were from an Egyptian exhibition on loan from Eton College and Durham University. Many pieces needed to be viewed through a magnifying glass, my favourite being a woman carrying a jar showing exquisite detail despite being only one inch in height. The MOA belief is that when art is good and beautiful it can bring healing to the body and the soul and enrich our daily lives by giving joy and a sense of purpose.

A Children's Art Exhibition is held here annually with participants from countries such as Portugal, Thailand, America, Brazil, Spain, Mexico, Argentina and Japan. This is a project to promote aesthetic education of the heart through beauty to assist in building character and strength in the children of today. In his speech at the 2007 Exhibition, Professor Tomoyoshi Endo, Minister of Education, Culture, Sports, Science and Technology, said:

"The important attribute of art is that it nurtures one's sensibility. Sensibility can be linked to people's hearts and minds. It's a feeling. People think and feel something is good, lovely, delightful or wonderful, when they see something beautiful. When we are able to feel something beautiful and to express such feelings in the form of a painting, a piece of calligraphy, a story or a poem, we cultivate our essential sentiment and sensibility. I believe that this could help to prevent crimes."

Modern-day scientists know the effects upon the human organism when exposed to beautiful art, flowers and lovely scenes in nature. Some documented results include raising the immune system, lowering blood pressure and switching the autonomous nervous system from the stressful sympathetic circuit to the restful, restorative parasympathetic circuit. Ancient cultures have always known this to be true and now science is saying that to bring beauty into our everyday lives is important in order to maintain health and wellbeing.

After leaving the Museum, we journeyed to the Ohito Training Centre where I received a warm welcome from the staff. Prior to leaving Australia, I had wondered whether I would see cherry blossoms in flower but that afternoon, I found myself sitting on a balcony overlooking a mountain of flowering blossoms, almost touching these delicate blooms.

Dinner was a unique experience held in a large dining area where floor-length glass gave the illusion of sitting in the beauty of nature. The ingredients used here are organic and grown at the MOA nature farms. I was interested to learn that research has shown it takes approximately three days of eating organically grown food for our taste buds to return to a normal healthy state. The food was prepared and served with love by highly qualified chefs. We now know the vibration of the person at the time of preparing food, whether positive or negative, is transmitted into the food. This was not a new concept to me as Poppy, a cook during the Second World War, prepared food to nourish battle-worn bodies and also believed the most important ingredient in any recipe was 'love'. "Itadakimasu" - gratitude to the food and the chefs was expressed before consuming a meal.

I slept soundly that night and felt welcome in this country that was far from my place of origin.

MY SOUL COUNTRY

Eating a wholesome breakfast lay the foundation for a new day that was to begin with a journey to the Oku-Atami Ryoin (Clinic).

Mokichi Okada had put together a comprehensive health and wellness structure to support the body's inherent self-healing powers. Based on these guidelines, the Oku-Atami Ryoin combines modern scientific methods with alternative approaches to restore optimum health. The doctor in charge welcomed our arrival before guiding us through this modern clinic constructed from natural materials and flowing with the essence of vitality and beauty. Vibrant timbers and polished floors showcased large glass windows overlooking acres of natural scenery and led to the medical/scientific part of the building, complete with modern facilities such as ex-ray equipment. We saw in-patient accommodation designed to support the body's self-healing abilities. The facility advocates lifestyle as being a major player in the onset of illness and says mental and emotional factors affect the disease progress. Treatment focuses on investigating the cause of disease from a physical and a psychological perspective as well as supporting the patient to introduce positive lifestyle changes.

I was then introduced to the Division of Okada Purifying Therapy. Developed by Mr Okada, it is a hands-on treatment to support the belief that physical and psychological disorders are not necessarily signs of physiological malfunction, but are viewed as a natural process of purification to restore balance to the body, purging it of toxins that lead to disease. In liaison with this Division is the MOA Health Science Centre, where scientific research is carried out into the effectiveness of the Okada Purifying Therapy. A certification process is in place for practitioners with ongoing overseeing of their training.

MOA also offers nutrition counselling based on dietary guidelines designed to change poor eating habits. They have adopted a term called, "utsukashiki" meaning beautiful, healthy, elegant and functional, but say that these terms do not properly describe its true meaning in the English language. Perhaps this is at the heart of MOA's teachings, the education of people so as to create healthy families through learning respect, value and mutual understanding. Creating a home that is happy and beautiful filled with the spirit of gratitude and valuing the interconnectedness of all life (MOA, 2006, p 16).

I was then welcomed to the Division of Horticulture Therapy by a graduate from the Kansas State University and an inspirational leader in her field. Horticultural therapy, used as a complementary treatment in the United States and other countries around the world, promotes health and wellbeing by improving the body and mind through gardening-related activities. The garden I experienced was grown and nurtured by the therapist and I was delighted to learn that all practitioners, including the medical doctors, were responsible for the creation of gardens surrounding their area of work.

MOA (2006, p 67) says, "When we hold a flower in our hands and become truly aware of its beauty, gazing at it as if we were talking with it, our suffering and afflictions are healed. Flowers possess a mysterious power to cleanse the human heart."

The MOA Museum of Art, I had visited the previous day, was but one section of the Art Division, others include flower arranging, tea ceremony, ceramics, music and the composition of poetry. My personal experience was the tea ceremony therapy. My heart wept with joy experiencing this sacred practice from a young practitioner, who was herself on the brink of motherhood.

MOA (2006, p 67) says, "A cup of tea prepared with sincere hospitality touches the heart of the person who receives and drinks it, awakening a sense of gratitude in him and promoting pleasant conversation."

However, the wonders of this day were not over. We journeyed onwards to explore the beauty of the Zuisenkyo and Ohito Farm founded on the Okada preventative health care concept and the belief that humans need to live in harmony with the laws of nature. At the nature farm many workers helped to create and maintain the acres of glorious gardens and hillsides once covered in scrubby terrain. MOA is a non-profit making organisation where people volunteer their time to experience the therapeutic effects of agriculture work and as a respite from the stress of modern lifestyle. This delightful experience ended with lunch at the restaurant, the highlight being a delicious wholesome ice cream, after which I was invited to explore the food store where a variety of organic produce filled with the vital sun, water and earth energy could be purchased. MOA have established these stores throughout Japan and supply nature lunches to the children of the MOA preschools, thereby providing daily healing for young bodies.

It was time to meet our guide who spoke little English. However, despite my Japanese speaking ability being very limited, I had the weirdest experience of not knowing whether he had spoken in English or Japanese as we understood each other very well. I felt like a queen that afternoon being guided through acres of flowers, a haven of beauty, healing and peace.

The Division of Nature Farming began over seventy years ago, and has facilities in many countries such as North and South America, Hawaii, Thailand and Taiwan. It does not use pesticides or chemical fertilisers, but seeks to maximise the life power of the soil. This method is in contrast to the chemicals used in modern agriculture that support pollution, drain natural resources and jeopardise the safety of human lives. The first consideration of this system is monetary profit in contrast to the MOA farmers who put the health of consumers before everything else and regard the soil as a living entity. As an example of this concept, MOA research has shown that crops grown continuously in the same soil increase in vitality and abundance. They say this can be likened to a person working in one area of expertise to become a specialist in his field.

Ancient Japanese wisdom (shindofuji) says, "The people and the soil are essentially one."

We spent a delightful afternoon exploring tea plantations, fields of crops and experiencing the beauty of hillsides transformed by human hands and my favourite, the animal farm. Here cows, pigs, sheep, chickens and rabbits live in a natural environment accepting respect and love as their birthright. Since leaving Australia, my experience had been everything Japanese and I was quite unprepared for my next discovery. On this farm in Japan far from the arid deserts of Australia were the most enormous emus, I had in memory witnessed seeing.

When saying farewell to our guide earlier that afternoon, I heard the words, "Come back, I'll be waiting." In that moment, I knew, I had found my soul country.

The World of Moss, Rock and Water

The next day we said farewell to the Training Centre; the chefs, their wondrous gift of healing food, the cherry blossom trees and the Oku-Atami Ryoin where I had experienced Okado Purifying Treatments. The drive to Hakone was shrouded in mist and I did not see Mt Fuji, Japan's holy volcano, from the lookout we visited, nor did I see Mt Fuji from the surrounds of Lake Ashi, a huge crater lake formed some four thousand years ago. I was not disappointed, however, as the volcano's watchful presence could be felt every step of the journey.

We escaped from the cold into the warmth of a nearby hotel to enjoy a steaming hot cup of coffee before continuing on our way to explore the Moss and Rock Garden. This famous tourist landmark had its beginning long ago when Mr Okada planted one piece of moss. Seven years later his place of beauty was complete, as people from all over Japan came to contribute moss, rock and helping hands. His home remains here today, a reminder that one man's vision beginning with one step can truly leave an inspiring legacy.

Although the facility was closed for the day, except for a garden tea party, I was to receive the privilege of a guided journey through this rich and vibrant landscape. Our guide was quick to point out that after falling rain is the best time to explore the garden. It had been raining all morning, but the sun appeared upon our arrival and remained until our departure, perhaps a sign that the sacred guardians welcomed our presence. There were no tourists, just myself, Tak, our guide and glimpses of elegant women attending a tea party in traditional dress. It was a moment in yestertime and I surrendered to the surreal world of moss, rock and water. When it was time to leave, my experience was then a fascinating trip through the streets of Hakone and a return to where our journey had begun.

The World of Beauty began with a vision and grew to the present-day wonder making one man's dream a reality that is a blueprint for a higher dimensional way of living; one we too can bring into our everyday lives.

PART THREE

Say Goodbye to Cancer

Glimpses of the work of loved teachers wind through this section and I give gratitude for their wisdom, knowledge and love. Principals of the two yoga schools where I studied for many happy years (both now deceased) and the work of Dr Patricia Sherwood, a phenomenological researcher, psychologist, author and lecturer.

CHAPTER 27

Body/Mind/Spirit Connection

"You cannot control the world outside,
but you can choose what you
will bring into yourself. If you do not see anything of value
in your life begin by growing a flower,
vegetable or tree every day
until it becomes a habit. You will discover much of value."

(Geoff Buckley, 2008)

At the time of writing, it is three years since hearing those words, "That's an angry breast." I have allowed the time to heal and rebuild from the fallout of a bumpy cancer journey and in hindsight, I am grateful for life experiences that have enabled me to gain an insight into modern-day stressors contributing to disease. I am also grateful for the knowledge gained to assist in rebalancing the physical, mental and emotional aspects of my being. I have learnt that nurturing the self is vital to wellbeing and a basis for any healing plan. The science of epigenetics tells us that our thoughts, emotions and environmental stressors, talk to our genes contributing towards the turning 'on' or turning 'off' genes with a predisposition to disease. Every positive thought and emotion can trigger the release of hormones to orchestrate the birthing of white cells, our immune system's foremost tool for fighting disease.

It has been shown that being in a beautiful place in nature or in the presence of someone who loves you or spending time in meditation can turn on health promoting genes. Peter Crook (2014) says, "Be still and silent for set periods in the day. This way, we learn to be in our own place and to be centred and present." Create a sacred space and this can be a seat in a corner of a garden or by placing a candle or something precious on a shelf.

The following tools can assist in this regard and to encourage you to seek further information on gentle, life-affirming techniques to bring into your wellness plan.

Body Talk

> Lie on your back with arms by your sides and palms facing upwards (a small pillow may be placed under your head). Alternatively, sit in a comfortable chair making sure the room is warm.

> Close your eyes and become aware of your body and the flow of the natural breath. Focus your attention on your feet, imagine the breath flowing through the feet and say, "Feet, please release tension and tightness." With the inhalation, feel the breath flowing into your feet and the negative energy leaving in the form of a grey smoke with each exhalation.

> Repeat this process, working through the body to release all tension. First, the ankles, then, shins, knees, thighs, pelvis, tummy, chest, throat, chin, cheeks, nose, eyes, forehead, top of the head, back of the head, back of the neck, shoulders, arms, hands, fingers, buttocks, back of the legs, the heels and the soles of the feet.

> When the body is completely relaxed, take your awareness to the breath, observe the natural inhalation and the exhalation. After a time, let go of breath awareness and allow the body to rest in that inner light of peace, harmony and tranquility.

> Become conscious of the part of the body holding disease such as a tumour in the right breast and speak to it saying what feels

right for you. For example, "Thank you for protecting me but you may no longer feed off my energy and I demand you leave."

Breathe into that part of the body and imagine the cancerous cells breaking up and leaving the body in the form of a grey smoke. Visualise what feels right for you and make it as creative as you wish. For example: believe that your breath can bring in a warrior of the light and visualise this being wielding a golden sword encouraging cancer cells to leave. Keep visualising and breathing until you feel an energetic shift.

When you are ready, use a sound to clear out the remaining debris - such as 'Shhhhhhh,' 'Zzzzzzzz,' 'Om,' or 'Hum,' - whatever comes into your thoughts will be perfect. Direct the sound to the space to be cleansed until it feels clear.

When we release something, we need to fill the space with a positive vibration.

Inhale whatever you need into where the tumour had been. Ask and know that whatever comes into your mind is right for you, for example, if the quality needed is peace, remember a time when you felt peace. Bring the memory of feeling peaceful into your body, breathe it into the place where the tumour had been and then breathe the feeling of peace from that space into every cell in your body. If you cannot remember such a moment, bring to mind someone who you believe has this quality, ask them to give the quality to you and see yourself receiving it. When this feels complete, remain in this place of peace for as long as you wish.

When you are ready, become aware of your body, wriggle your toes and fingers, stretch your arms over your head, stretch and stretch. Curl up into a foetal position, give yourself a hug and know that you are a ball of peace.

(If you have difficulty moving your body, do this in your imagination and know that it is so).

EARTH, AIR, FIRE AND WATER MEDICINE

Combining fire, water and earth contact with conscious breathing is an excellent recipe for regaining balance and health. Listen to your body and know that even five minutes of each exercise per day will be a good foundation on which to build health.

Air

Breathing Meditation: Breathe well to live well.

> Lie in a comfortable position (or sit in a comfortable chair), your feet flopping out to the sides and your palms facing upwards. Gently close your eyes and move your awareness around the body consciously inhaling into each part holding tension, letting it go with each exhalation. Feel yourself becoming more and more relaxed and rest in the calm stillness, the place where your inner physician resides.

> Let go of body awareness and become aware of your thoughts. Allow them to flutter across the screen of your mind like a flock of birds flying across the sky. Have no involvement, watch them come and watch them go. After a time, take your attention to feelings or emotions and having no involvement, allow the sensations to rise and dissipate.

> Now, becoming aware of the natural breath - the gentle inhalation and the exhalation flowing into the pause at the end of the breath. Breathe slow and deep into the belly allowing it to move freely as the breath flows through your whole being. Become the silent witness, watch the body being breathed.

> When you are ready, let go of breath awareness and become conscious of the room you are in, the sounds within the room, the sounds outside and stretch and stretch. Curl up into a foetal position, give yourself a hug and give gratitude for your body, your breath and your life.

Fire

Consciously greet the sun upon rising, allowing its light to set your daily rhythm so as to be in tune with the natural cycle of the day. Sit with bare feet touching the earth or lie on the earth feeling the warm healing rays of the sun invigorating every cell in your body. Know that this is the highest vibrational food, activating positive genes and orchestrating health and vitality. Up to twenty minutes every day with as much skin exposure as possible will be most beneficial.

Light a candle and gently gaze upon its vibrant dance with focused concentration. Close your eyes and see the shimmering after image, returning your gaze again and again to the flame.

When snuggling up in front of a fire, watch the dance of the flames. Gaze through soft eyes and know that you are a witness to their storytelling.

Water

Drink six to eight glasses of pure water every day - half an hour before taking meals and then approximately two-and-a-half hours after each meal. Drink more water around the heaviest meal and a small glass before bedtime (Batmanghelidj, 2008).

After skin brushing (see Chapter 28) take a warm shower or soak in a bath with Epsom salts or pure essential oils (to suit your own health regime) - light candles, play ambient music. Imagine the water washing away physical, emotional and mental toxins.

> Spend time in and near water. When lying on the sand at the beach imagine a wave washing over your body and up to your chin. See and feel toxins, tensions and worries leave your body with the wave as it recedes back into the ocean. Become aware of the soft sand cradling your body and the warm sun energising your body, breathe in the oxygen rich air and visualise the prana (life force energy) flowing into your body, healing and revitalising every cell.

Earth

Walk every day, if possible.

Spend time lying on the earth or sit with your bare feet touching the earth. Admire nature's beauty or potter in the garden and touch living soil.

Visit natural environments, appreciate nature and know that she is appreciating you.

Grounding

When feeling spacey, anxious or fearful, connecting to the earth can assist you to be present in the body. This can be done anywhere but to walk barefoot on the earth is ideal, especially when the grass is tingling with morning dew. Our bodies are wise and take in exactly the right number of electrons needed to counteract free radicals. Leather or hide shoes allow contact with the earth, whilst modern footwear blocks this important flow of energy.

Bend your knees and feel the contact with the earth while inhaling deeply, allowing the breath to fill the whole body.

Exhale feelings such as spacey, anxious or fearful and see them flowing out of the toes in the form of a grey smoke and into the earth.

Inhale the earth energy through the soles of the feet bringing feelings such as calm, connectedness and strength into the whole body.

Repeat until feeling more grounded and say, "I am calm, connected and strong."

Give gratitude to the Earth.

Grounding Visualisation

Lie in a comfortable position with palms facing upwards. Close your eyes and inhale and exhale deeply and slowly. Say, "Let go, give in." Mentally scan your body for tightness or tension and release with the breath until your whole body is feeling relaxed.

Inhale into the heart and become aware of the feelings you wish to release, letting them go with each and every exhalation. Take your time and when you feel an energy shift, inhale whatever quality, such as joy, peace or happiness, you need in this moment. Remember a time when you had experienced having this quality and inhale the feeling, allowing it to flow into every cell in your body. When you are feeling relaxed and balanced, remain in that place of inner calm and be mindful of just being in the moment.

When you are ready, bring your awareness to the place between the eyebrows and know that you can take your consciousness to wherever you want. In your mind's eye visualise a beautiful place in nature - the grass is green, the sky blue, the sun warm and nurturing, the water in a nearby stream is clear and sparkling. Listen to the playful breeze rustling the leaves of nearby trees and water falling gently over smooth brown rocks. Inhale nature's perfume and walk on the green grass, breathing the earth's energy up through the soles of your feet, feeling it flow into your body, bringing calm and balance. Feel a gentle breeze touching your cheek and hear the birds' song.

Removing your clothes, leave them on a nearby rock and feel the sun's warm rays on your skin. Enter the water and feel the cool liquid drops washing over you, purifying and cleansing your whole body. Become one with the water allowing it to cradle your body as you float on this calm watery bed, feeling safe and protected.

Return to the bank in your own time. Feel the sun's healing rays warm your body and the earth's balancing energy flowing up through the soles of your feet. Inhale deeply and bring an awareness of the joy of this wondrous place in nature into your whole being. Give gratitude for your life and know that you can return to this sacred place any time you wish. All you have to do is close your eyes.

In your own time, prepare to leave. Allow the breath to deepen, become aware of your body and the room you are in, open your eyes and stretch and stretch.

Ho'oponopono

Dr Masaru Emoto's famous experiments showed the effect of thought and word on water. Beautiful crystals form when words such as "I love you" or "thank you" are spoken whilst muddy, malformed crystals are the result when water is subjected to negative words such as, "You fool". As the human body is made up of approximately seventy percent water (eighty percent for a young child and sixty percent for an elderly person), his work shows the power of thought and word on our internal environment. I once heard the metaphysician, Stuart Wilde, comment that we are walking puddles of water! Thoughts and words are like magic wands often used with little awareness of their true power. However, this is not always the case. Many traditional people use the power of words through rituals and an example is Ho'oponopono, an ancient Hawaiian teaching.

Ho'o means to 'make' and pono is translated as 'right', meaning everything is in its right place and right time. This healing wisdom is about taking responsibility for ourselves and releasing the fears and worries that create a blockage in the flow of energy throughout the body. These can manifest as illness on a cellular level. Ulrich Dupree (2012, p 18) writes, "Sicknesses are seen as symptoms of inner conflict, and the energetic tensions are released through a shamanistic Ho'oponopono ritual. When the soul is healed, the body follows."

Ho'oponopono was brought to the attention of the world by the work of Dr Ihaleukala Hew Len, a psychiatrist who worked in the psychiatric department of the state prison of Kaneohe in Hawaii. He found the inmates chronically mentally ill and the staff not equipped to cope with the hellish situation they faced every day. Dr Hew Len set about reading the patients' files on a regular basis and at the same time, searching within his heart for bits of the reflected darkness he saw in those pages of horror, such as power, envy or aggression. He prayed with intent and feeling, "I love you. I'm sorry. Forgive me. Thank you." After four years, the institution was closed and all except two of the prisoners were healed.

Dr Ihaleukala Hew Len took responsibility for the prisoners in his life who were showing him fragments of negative self-talk and dark thinking lingering in his heart. He acknowledged outdated familial, societal or religious teachings and beliefs, replacing them with life-supporting information. Affirmations repeated over and over may not be successful if a subconscious programme is firmly entrenched saying the opposite is true. We may not know why this is so but our outer world will always be a perfect mirror. Dr Francesca Rossetti (1992, p 74) wrote, "The 15th century physician Paracelsus knew that there was a good reason why a particular patient was attracted to visit him for treatment. He looked within himself for the answer, rectifying the imbalances which he discerned within the patient, realising that if he initially worked on himself there would be a greater inner connection and therefore response between himself and the patient."

It was Joe Vitale (2007) who brought Dr Hew Len's work to the attention of Western culture. He says Dr Hew Len taught him that when we say Ho'oponopono with intent, we are cleaning the 'old beliefs', the programmes we share. It is then up to the Divine who is already showering us with the love that old disjointed patterns are keeping us from experiencing.

"I love you - I'm sorry - Forgive me - Thank you."

During a session with the kinesiologist, my body memory went to the time when my grandmother passed over with cancer. When brought to my attention, vivid memories of what happened could be recalled even though I had been but seven years of age. My mother reinforced the beliefs taken on at that time by repeatedly telling the family story of my grandmother's passing. This became a page in the book of my life and went on to become a factor in my cancer story today. However, I believe that by clearing this story from the cells of the body, there has been little intrusion from outdated beliefs that may have otherwise sabotaged the healing process. We do not have to sit in therapy for years to do this as change can happen quickly. I have experienced this not only through kinesiology but through body-based psychotherapy and artistic therapies such as art, music, dance and clay. These modalities speak the language of the soul and open the doorway to the heart.

When Dr Masaru Emoto (2003, pp 147-150) froze water crystals exposed to electromagnetic frequencies from microwave ovens, cell phones, televisions and computers, they formed horrible shapes. However, when sending thoughts of 'love' and 'gratitude' the water crystals formed were more whole, suggesting that the impact of a positive over a negative is very powerful. We do not have to accept negative thought forms acquired throughout our lives and stored within the cells of our bodies. When recognised, these can be transformed to a positive vibration.

There is salvation. It is called, love and gratitude.

THE JAPANESE MAPLE TREE

I am looking at a Japanese maple tree guarding the entry to my home and through its thinning branches peep bits of orange sun. As I write, golden leaves flutter past the large picture window, each one offering a blessing. Soon it will be bare, the leaves of today will become the compost of tomorrow and then in a little while, green shoots will appear and once again it will wear a new dress. Ah, the never-ending cycle of life unfolds before my eyes, the stories it could tell, my own but a small book in the great library past from tree to tree over time. How fortunate I am to have such a friend.

The shedding of its leaves is like the releasing of old tears, its bared branches, a metaphor for where I find myself at this moment. However, in time I will also feel new life stirring and like my guardian tree, I too will wear a new dress. The old will be gone, the time for renewal will come and with it, a new cycle flowing with the never-ending dance of life.

When I hug my tree it graciously transmutes my angst. I come away feeling a little lighter for having experienced the gift of the sun 's light flowing through its branches and the earth's dark pulsing energy flowing through its roots. I am a little more balanced, whole and peaceful because I have a friend and guardian, a Japanese maple tree.

TREE MEDITATION

Lie in a comfortable position with your body straight, palms facing upwards or sit in a comfortable chair or with your back up against a real live tree.

Become aware of your breath. Inhale slowly and deeply into your belly and when exhaling, say, "Giving in, letting go."

Move your consciousness around your body letting go of any tension or tightness until the whole body is relaxed and say, "Whole body relaxed."

Visualise a beautiful place in nature - a forest dell, green grass, blue sky, sunlight on the leaves of the trees - make it whatever you wish.

Feel your feet walking on the grass, the sun on your skin, the caress of a gentle breeze on your face. Smell the crisp clean air, hear the sounds of the birds and the little creatures of the forest.

Take a moment to enjoy the variety of trees surrounding your dell and become aware of one that stands out and is perhaps calling you. See its branches reaching up to the sky and the roots going down into the earth.

Sit with your back against the tree's trunk and feel its strength. Speak to your tree and listen to what it says. Ask permission to receive its gifts.

Look up at the branches reaching towards the sky. Feel the sun's warm rays flowing down the branches into the crown of your head and your whole body. Breathe in the nourishing light from Father Sun.

Bring to mind a quality that you believe you need at this time, one a father figure in your life would give to you, such as strength, protection and courage. Visualise Father Sun giving it to you and feel it flowing down through the branches of the tree into every organ and cell in your body. Inhale deeply and slowly and believe you are this quality.

Press your back into the trunk of the tree, feel its support and see the strong roots going down into the ground, connecting with the Earth Mother. Feel her loving energy flowing up through the roots and into your feet as you breathe in this nurturing energy.

Bring to mind a quality that you believe you need at this time, one a mother figure in your life would give to you, such as love, trust and warmth. Visualise the Earth Mother giving it to you and feel it flowing up through the earth into every organ and cell in your body. Inhale deeply and slowly and believe you are this quality.

When you are ready, press your back into the trunk of the tree and breathe into the heart centre, feeling balanced, whole, loved and supported. Remain in this space of love for as long as you wish and when you leave, know that you can return any time you wish, all you have to do is close your eyes.

Thank your tree for the blessings you have been given, open your eyes and stretch and stretch.

If you feel inclined, draw or paint a picture of your tree and place it where you can constantly gaze upon it to reinforce the qualities received in your meditation.

LAUGHING YOGI

In my years of teaching yoga, I have not given the following exercise without everyone rolling on the floor laughing. I often had a picture of myself laughing and no-one joining in but it did not happen. Happiness is a natural state of being, so getting into the habit of laughing is a great idea. Resulting from this practice, I have seen deep belly laughter which is something we have almost forgotten how to do.

Laughter 'turns on' positive switches in our bodies and floods our cells with feel good chemicals that lift our vibration and press the 'heal' button. People laughing, whistling and singing is a childhood memory that makes me smile to this very day. It has been said that five minutes of laughter can activate the immune system and this positivity can remain with us for up to twenty-four hours.

Laugh, whistle and sing to turn on the 'heal' button.

This is soul medicine. If those dark wings of fear come flapping, no matter how hard it seems, take your awareness to something beautiful, a flower, a picture, the falling rain, whatever makes you smile. Something I try to do at these times is to walk barefoot in nature, feeling the sun's warmth filling those dark holes of despair. Remember, you can do this in your mind, you can always smile, chuckle and yes, even laugh, no matter what.

MEDITATION

Kneel on the floor, bring the toes together and separate the heels. Lower the buttocks to rest between the feet. Alternatively, you may sit in a chair. Yawn, stretch your arms over your head and then bring your hands to rest on the knees. Remember to use slow conscious movements.

Release any tension and tightness by rotating your awareness around the body, breathing into each part and letting go.

Inhale while gently drawing your shoulders up towards the head. Feel the tension in the shoulder and neck area. Let it go as you exhale and slowly return your shoulders to their original position.

Smile and bend forward from the waist, bringing your forehead towards the floor. Smile and feel your body smiling. Say, "My body is smiling," and slowly return to a sitting position.

Chuckle and bend forward from the waist. Chuckle and feel your body chuckling. Say, "My body is chuckling," and slowly return to a sitting position.

Laugh and bend forward from the waist.

Laugh with your body and allow laughter to flow into every cell in your body, let go, laugh with abandon, feel the whole body laughing.

Tumeric Tea

2 knobs of the turmeric root or 1 teaspoon of powdered turmeric

1 knob of ginger root

A slice of lemon

Honey to sweeten

A sprinkle of ground black pepper (helps to absorb the turmeric and to enhance the effectiveness)

Add boiling water and allow to stand for 5-10 minutes

Enjoy

Turmeric has been shown by scientific research to have natural health-promoting properties and is known to be a powerful anti-inflammatory and anti-cancer substance. It is widely used as a spice in traditional dishes in many cultures where its health-giving gift is recognised. For instance, in India where it is widely used, prostate, colon, breast and lung cancers show a marked decline in comparison to Western countries. Curcumin, a component of turmeric, is considered to be the major contributory factor.

The www.greenmedinfo.com website contains an extensive database on the subject of turmeric's medical value. You will find research on turmeric's potential to assist in prevention and/or treatment of drug resistant cancers, chronic degenerative conditions, neurological problems, depression, serious infections, as well as hundreds of other diseases. Turmeric is said to protect cells against oestrogen-like chemicals and it is highly regarded in Ayurvedic and Traditional Chinese Medicine.

CHAPTER 28

Medicine List a Blueprint for Health

LIFESTYLE MEDICINE

TREATMENT PROGRAMME - with the support of qualified practitioners who have knowledge and experience in working with the chosen therapies.

SUPPLEMENTS - with the support of a qualified practitioner of natural medicine who has an understanding of the cancer journey and can determine your individual needs; someone who has knowledge of what is required to support you through Western therapies if needed and of when supplements are given so as not to interfere with these treatments. A practitioner who can determine whether the supplements you are taking are working for your body and in unison. Like an orchestra when one instrument is playing out of tune, if one supplement is out of sync, everything can be undermined.

DIET - eat food that is locally grown in season, paddock to plate if possible, and then prepared with love. Avoid genetically modified, chemically laden, pre-packaged, fast, sugar laden food. Consider a whole-foods, plant-based diet, drink approximately six to eight glasses of purified chemical free water and juice raw vegetables on a daily basis. Always hydrate upon rising. Show love to self by choosing healthy eating habits.

RELAXED EATING - mindful, relaxed, slow eating is important for digestion and assimilation of food to obtain the maximum benefit. Hurried eating in a stressful environment such as watching the news is a stressor to our body. Stressors turn off the digestion and assimilation process. The pleasure experienced when eating a meal rich in taste and aroma improves digestion.

HOLISTIC DENTISTRY- a wise precaution is to find the support of a holistic or biological dentist who can determine what work needs to be done to lessen toxicity to the body. Teeth are alive and respond to daily oral care such as oil pulling, salt rinsing, tongue scraping and the use of essential oils. Reference to oil pulling can be found in Ayurvedic texts that date back fifteen thousand years and support its use as a powerful detoxification method, removing bacteria, reducing plaque and tightening the gums. It is best to avoid mouth washes and toothpastes containing harmful chemicals and fluoride that can kill the good bacteria and burn the gums.

EMF'S AND CHEMICALS - have an awareness of electromagnetic frequencies and environmental chemicals and lessen exposure where possible. Indirect EMF and chemical protection include regular relaxation periods, exercise, eating a natural organic diet, safe, regular sun exposure and earthing. We are all sensitive to electromagnetic radiation to varying degrees and therefore, protecting your energy field and cleaning your environment is important.

EARTH, AIR, FIRE AND WATER HEALING - have regular and conscious exposure to sunlight, the earth, fresh air and water roaming freely in nature, such as the seaside or a running brook. Barefoot contact with the Earth is important.

EXERCISE - include daily exercise such as walking, swimming and/or gentle no strain exercise such as yoga, Tai Chi or Qigong that balance the body. The use of a rebounder (mini-trampoline) has proven health benefits including increased oxygen intake and lymphatic system support. Regular use of a Chi machine is a gentle way to support the lymphatic system.

BREATHING - slow, deep breathing to increase oxygen intake and to release physical, emotional and mental toxicity can take you to that place of inner calm and balance. To oxygenate and detox, include diaphragmatic or belly breathing, a living food diet and lots of movement into your daily regime. Slow, deep, relaxed breathing activates the parasympathetic nervous system bringing relief from stress and improving health, vitality and longevity.

REST - listen to your body and have plenty of rest when needed. Sleeping in a dark room is important as light disrupts the production of melatonin and if this occurs regularly, health issues including a breast cancer risk can increase. Melatonin production spikes between the hours of ten and two o'clock. Grandma's adage, 'early to bed and early to rise', is wisdom.

LIFESTYLE - become aware of lifestyle practices such as alcohol consumption and smoking and make changes accordingly. Small gradual changes have an effect on every part of our being and lead to a healthier outcome.

SKIN BRUSHING - to encourage oxygen and nutrient flow to the cells, the removal of toxins and dead skin cells via the bloodstream and lymphatic system. Begin at the feet and brush upwards towards the heart, excluding the face, nipples, broken skin or varicose veins. Use a dry long-handled natural bristle brush, have a hot shower afterwards and rehydrate with pure water. Gentle skin brushing can be an excellent way to enliven the body when feeling tired.

INFRARED SAUNA - a safe way to remove toxins, rebalance from electromagnetic frequency disruption and to gently exercise the body, boost immunity, balance body alkalinity and to activate the relaxation response. Although not as potent as hyperthermia it is nevertheless, a gentle way to raise the body heat. Cancer cells are sensitive to heat and can be destroyed by high temperatures leaving normal cells intact. It is important to stay hydrated and to replenish with minerals during the process whilst eating lots of green leafy vegetables to enhance the detoxification process.

FOREST BATHING - spend time in a forest and mindfully breathe, walk, see, feel and hear. Sitting in silence, under a tree is perfect. Have no thoughts or expectations, just be in the stillness of the moment. This is a wonderful healing science to boost immunity and release toxins from the physical, emotional, mental and spiritual aspects of ourselves.

HUGGING - a loving physical connection has been scientifically shown to positively affect every cell in the body, boost the immune response and to be food for the heart. So, hug those you love, a pet or your favourite tree and feel that heart to heart connection. Curl up into a foetal position and hug yourself, smiling into your heart and your whole body.

SELF-FIRST - adopt a gentle nurturing lifestyle. Conscious living leads to quality of life, longevity and a peaceful passing when the time comes to walk into the silence of tomorrow.

SAY 'NO' - no more pleasing others as it is time to live your truth, stay in your power and honour yourself.

LISTEN - to your inner guidance, that silent witness.

SELF-TALK - be aware of self-talk, the voices within from pre-conditioning and learn to change the script or seek the support of a body-mind therapist to release negative cellular memory. Become aware of when you are not in your body, thinking about the future, worrying about the past and not experiencing the moment. Allow pure consciousness to flow as this is the true healer.

SHOCKS TO THE BODY- become aware of life situations that may have left blocked energy within the body and remove with the support of a body-mind therapist, such as a kinesiologist, holistic counsellor or homeopath.

NEGATIVITY - have an awareness of negativity such as television-talk and people who leave you feeling drained (emotional vampires). Play soothing music that resonates with your heart, let the answering machine take your calls and forget the guilt trip if you do not ring back.

SUPPORT TEAM - time to keep only those who truly have your best interests at heart, as you no longer have the energy to carry others who are dumping old worn out dramas onto you. It is important that your support circle has an understanding of the treatment plan and can put your wellbeing before self-interest. Unresolved issues that poison the body and negative relationships can undermine a treatment plan. Healing, repairing and rebuilding is a slow process.

BEAUTY - surround yourself and your home environment in beauty and take Aunt Marg's vase that makes you cringe to a local charity shop. Science can now verify the positive effect on body, mind and emotions of looking at a beautiful picture or a scene in nature and the negative effect of say, watching a violent movie or a news flash on television. If you are in bed or in a hospital, create a beautiful scene in your mind and go there regularly with the drips, the beeping technology, the pain and just 'be'. It is where you are at the moment and it will pass. As Aron says, "It is what it is." However, the vase has to go!

ASK - for assistance when needed and accept with gratitude what is offered to you.

STRESS - we know that stress plays a significant part in disease so stressful people, places and situations can no longer be a part of your life. Learn relaxation techniques to bring the body to a balanced state of being. Stress is a toxin causing inflammation and adds to our load of acidity.

LAUGHTER - is a great medicine and can release happy chemicals into the body to strengthen immunity. Watch a funny movie or simply do the Laughing Yogi Meditation (Chapter 27). Laugh at yourself. Remember the Irish proverb - "A good laugh and a long sleep are the best cures in the doctor's book."

JOY- include in your day something that makes your heart sing such as gazing into a flower, watching the wind rustling the leaves, listening to a loved one laugh or picking up the telephone and telling someone you love them. Feeling loved and giving love is perhaps our greatest healing tool. If you are feeling alone, remember a time when you felt loved, recapture the feeling and imagine that person giving it to you. Breathe it into every cell in your body until you are tingling with love.

SPIRITUAL MEDICINE

A NEW DAY - begin each day as a new beginning and give gratitude to complement your personal belief system, such as a saying a prayer. If you wake with negative thoughts racing, then use a technique such as Ho'oponopono, "I love you, I'm sorry, forgive me, thank you." Know that you are wiping away those 'sorry thoughts'. Replace with a positive affirmation and vision for the day ahead. Remember Victor Frankl's message saying that we have a choice as to our attitude when handling whatever we are experiencing. This may not be easy, but by having the fortitude to keep on keeping on and by bringing in positivity, magic can happen. Be gentle and loving with yourself.

LONG-TERM GOAL (A FUTURE VISION) - a reason to live, perhaps to see a child or grandchild grow and graduate, something that is so important that it makes your heart sing by just giving it thought. I believe it takes a coming together of many triggers for cancer cells to flourish. I look for answers, but at the end of the day what is more important is how I live my life in this moment. Whether I am here for a few months or many years, I strive to ensure that the time will be filled with conscious living. As Thea said, "A gift of cancer for me is that I can now feel emotion, the good and the bad - the joy, happiness, pain, fear. As a child, my heart closed, I couldn't feel, but now I can and that's exciting because I'm living. To experience it all is to be alive in the moment."

MEDITATION - can be lying on a mat, watching a bird fly, the fluttering of leaves in trees, walking with awareness or sitting in your favourite chair, just being with you. To make time each day to quieten the body and allow the inner dialogue to cease can become a cornerstone to your healing. It is during these moments that connection can be made to whatever you perceive the Divine to be. It is a time when the gifts of the spirit, such as beauty, grace and love can flow through every cell in your body.

CHOCOLATE CAKE - A friend baked me a chocolate cake. It was round, covered in chocolate icing with whole cherries adorning the top. His face beamed when he cut the slices, the cake itself was like a beaming face and I indulged in one slice. This was a time not long after my operation when my diet was rigid and I was trying to do everything 'right' for my recovery. The love put into the making of the cake shone from every bit of its chocolate ingredients and shared with two people I love, it was the best medicine. For its homeopathic properties of love, friendship, caring and endurance (how I relate to these friends) are still mine just for the want of 'seeing' that cake in my mind's eye. When I do, my heart smiles. What better spiritual medicine could there be? Friendship is perhaps one of the greatest blessings we will encounter on our spiritual journey into the heart, the place where grace resides and peace is home.

Make your medicine list as creative as you like for there are many healing techniques, such as flower essences, singing, dancing, crystals and essential oils. It has been said that there is no pure essential oil that does not have a beneficial cancer effect due to the oil's anti-inflammatory and antioxidant properties. Frankincense has been shown to be a natural cancer treatment and a drop of myrrh or sandalwood on the back of the neck boasts health benefits. It must be remembered, however, that only the purest oils are to be used and it is also wise to cultivate an awareness of what feels good for you. Taking time each day to pause, give gratitude and flow with nature's cycles are basic requirements. Choose to love what you do and choose the culture of life.

When a diagnosis is made, time is important, however there is never the urgency to rush into surgery the following day. There are many options available and worth considering. Time is important, but to be used to put together the best support team possible and with their input, a medicine list that suites you, the cancer, envisaged recovery and a goal of long-term quality living. You are unique, your cancer is unique and so should be your plan for recovery. Nobody resonates on the energy vibration that you do and cancer is a result of everyday living, thinking and feeling.

Your cancer experience will touch the lives of everyone you are connected to and some you do not even know. Celebrate your life for there is honour in living through such an experience and let no-one take away the right to make your decisions, put you down or make you feel in any way a failure. You have metaphorically speaking, climbed mountains, swum seas and survived. It is time for a new adventure and being in the moment of the now. Change is happening with every breath, so climb into the carriage, take the reins and be the silent witness steering those horses to a destiny that is uniquely yours. Only you have that connection and when the time comes to walk into the silence of tomorrow, your heart will guide the way. It is a well-known journey, be not afraid, nor doubt that it is so.

PART FOUR

Books, Documentaries and Websites that may be of Interest

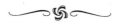

CHAPTER 29

Toxins bio-accumulate in our bodies and come from sources such as man-made chemicals polluting our air, water and soil, genetically modified food, electromagnetic frequencies, radiation and toxic adjuvants and preservatives found in vaccines. An individual predisposition coupled with a lifestyle-stressor that places the body into toxic overload can then open the way to a disease state. Having an awareness of and lessening these toxic stressors in our lives is paramount to maintaining wellness. This section contains information on scientists, practitioners and authors who perhaps have a piece of the puzzle to finding that pathway to a better way.

BOOKS/DOCUMENTARIES

Ausubel, K.

When Healing Becomes a Crime - The Amazing Story of the Hoxsey Cancer Clinics and the Return of Alternative Therapies.
Ausubel Kenny is the producer of several award-winning documentaries including *Hoxsey: How Healing Becomes a Crime.* This film won the Best Censored Stories award for investigative journalism. www.topdocumentaryfilms.com/ hoxsey-how-healing-becomes-a-crime.

Bijlsma, N.

Healthy Home Healthy Family - in the past twenty years ADHD and childhood allergies have increased by four hundred percent, one in four children now have asthma and autism has increased from one in every 10,000 live births to one in every 166 births. Breast cancer has more than doubled since the 1960's, the age of puberty is dramatically declining, sperm count has dropped by fifty percent and IVF is where you go to have children. Could these conditions be linked to the homes in which we live? www.buildingbiology.com.au.

Bollinger, T.

Cancer Step Outside the Box - a well-researched book.
The Truth About Cancer: What You Need to Know About Cancer's History, Treatment and Prevention. This book has been written for one simple reason: to share the knowledge we need to protect ourselves, treat ourselves, and in some cases, save our lives or the lives of those we love.

The Truth About Cancer - A Global Quest - a brilliant documentary series and the ideal place to begin your journey. Information on safe and effective cancer treatments and the doctors who are having success in this regard - a must see. www.cancertruth.net.

Bond, L.

Mum's NOT Having Chemo - a great book containing a -wealth of information to assist those putting together a road-map to healing from cancer. www.mumsnothavingchemo.com.

Coates, K. and Perry, V.

Embracing the Warrior - An Essential Guide for Women
Reclaim your health and vitality through the power of nutrition, movement and informed choice. www.drKaren.com.au.

Crook, P.

It Just Is
Just Be Quiet
You're Okay just the way you are
The Lightness of Life Without Thinking
The Illusion of Change and the Meaning of Acceptance
Power of Affection
Just Be Quiet - the Power of Silence
www.petercrookacupuncture.com.au.

Ellis, K.

Shattering the Cancer Myth - This is a unique positive guide to cancer treatment using traditional and natural therapies. It contains a wealth of information on herbal, dietary and supplement information as well as Katrina Ellis' story on how she pulled together traditional cancer treatments and natural therapies using skills as a naturopath to regain her health and become cancer free. www.katrinaellis.com.au.

Fischer, W.

How to Fight Cancer and Win - Scientific guidelines and documented facts for the successful treatment and prevention of cancer and other related health problems. Contains valuable information on the Budwig diet p. 129-185.

Fortson, L.

Embrace, Release, Heal - Following three cancer diagnosis in three years, Leigh Fortson was given few options by her doctors and little hope for a bright future, however, she changed everything. This is her story with valuable knowledge gained along the way to becoming healed. www.embracehealingcancer.com.

Gentempo, P.

Vaccines Revealed: The Biggest Public Health Experiment ... Ever, Interviews with leading vaccine authorities including Robert F. Kennedy Jr. (World Mercury Project), the documentary film, *Trace Amounts* and a preview of *Vaxxed - from cover-up to catastrophe*. Vaccines are part of the cancer story - a must watch. www.vacinesrevealed.com.

Griffin, G. Edward

World Without Cancer – The Story of Vitamin B17. G. Edward Griffin is a writer, documentary film producer, and founder of Freedom Force International. www.freedomforceinternational.org.

Heckenlively, K. and Mikovits, J.

Plague: One Scientist's Intrepid Search for the Truth About Human Retroviruses, Chronic Fatigue Syndrome (ME/CFS), Autism and Other Diseases. Groundbreaking work in epigenetics, virology and the nature of retroviral infection. www.plaguethebook.com.

Hillary, E.

Beyond the Toxic Harvest - A chemical poisoning survivor story. *Sarah's Last Wish* - A story of forced medicine. www.sarahs-last-wish.com.

Johnson, B.	*No Ma'am-ograms – Radical Rethink on Mammograms* - dispels the myths and sheds light on the truth of mammograms. Offering safer solutions to addressing prevention, diagnosis and treatment. *The Secret of Health: Breast Wisdom* - written with Kathleen Barnes. Drbenmd.com.
Lantz, S.	*Chemical Free Kids - raising healthy children in a toxic world.* Every parent should have this book. *Less Toxic Living.* www.chemicalfreeparenting.com.
Mercola, J.	*Sun Exposure Benefits and Safety Report* - free download www.mercola.com.downloads/bonus/benefits-of-sun-exposure/report.htm.
Moritz, A.	*Cancer is Not a Disease - it's a survival mechanism* - Discover cancer's hidden purpose, heal its root causes and be healthier than ever. www.ener-chi-com.

O'Bryan, T.

Autoimmune Fix - the latest science takes 17 years to trickle down to clinical practice - the excessive inflammation story is an initiator of degenerative processing leading to disease such as cancer. Cancer has autoimmune components in the initiating and fuelling stages. An important book. theDr.com.

Pierce, T.

Outsmart Your Cancer - is an excellent source of information on natural medicines and includes a scientific detailed account of how Protocel works as well as successful case studies from all age groups, including children. Protocel is the work of Jim Sheridan, targeting the anaerobic aspect of cancer cells while leaving healthy cells unharmed. Ms Pierce commented, "As much as I was amazed by the effectiveness of other alternative non-toxic approaches to cancer, I was stunned by the results of a brown liquid called, Protocel." Her website offers valuable information: www.outsmartyourcancer.com.

Smith, J.

Genetic Roulette - The Documented Health Risks of Genetically Engineered Foods - based on research, a chilling reminder that the effects of GM foods on human health are largely untested.

Seeds of Deception - Exposing Industry and Government Lies about the Safety of the Genetically Engineered Foods You're Eating.

www.secretingredientsmovie.com.
www.geneticroullettemovie.com.
www.ResponsibleTechnology.org.
www.genethics.org.
www.seedsofdeception.com.

Smith, R. and Lourie, B.

Slow Death by Rubber Duck - how the toxicity of everyday products impacts our health and wellbeing - an important book.

Toxin Toxout - advice for removing toxic chemicals from our bodies and homes.

www.toxintoxout.ca.

Cyber Information

Burrell, Lloyd	*How to Beat Electrical Sensitivity* - E-book - Lloyd Burrell has spent the past ten years researching the effects of electromagnetic fields on health. www.electricSense.com.
Campaign for Safe Cosmetics	Is my lipstick safe? - Visit here to find out. www.safecosmetics.org.
Environmental Working Group	EWG's mission is to conduct original, game-changing research that inspires people, businesses and governments to take action to protect human health and the environment. An excellent source of safe product and food guidelines: for example, the Dirty Dozen and the Clean 15. www.ewg.org.
Food Revolution Network	Envision a world where all people have access to enough affordable healthy wholesome food and clean water to meet their basic needs - a world in which governments are accountable to their people and manage essential resources sustainably. www.foodrevolution.org.

Genostics Testing	Gene profiling. CTC (circulating tumour cells) identification and monitoring tests. CTC analysis to assist with how a cancer will respond to radiotherapy, chemotherapy, botanicals and nutrients. Agents for South East Asia, China, India, Australia and New Zealand. www.genostics.com.au.
Havas, M	Associate professor of environmental and resource studies at Trent University, Canada, Dr Havas teaches and researches the biological effects of environmental contaminants. www.magdahavas.com.
International Medical Council on Vaccination	International Medical Council on Vaccination is an association of medical doctors, registered nurses and other qualified medical professionals whose purpose is to counter the messages asserted by pharmaceutical companies, the government and medical agencies that vaccines are safe, effective and harmless. Our conclusions have been reached individually by each member of the Council, after thousands of hours of personal research, study and observation. www.vaccinationcouncil.org.

Simoncini, T.

Cancer is a Fungus - Dr Simoncini says that cancer is a fungal infection on the outside of the cell. Using intravenous sodium bicarbonate, he claims a seventy to eighty percent success rate when patients are not terminal or have metastasis. www.cancerfungus.com.

Thermography & thermology

The American College of Clinical Thermology - information on thermology and thermography and where to find ACCT approved thermography clinics worldwide. www.thermologyonline.org.

Epilogue

CELEBRATION

Twelve months on from the operation, I am running a children's programme for a local festival held once a year to showcase local business and promote regional sustainable eating. I was exhausted at the end of a long day, my fuzzy chemo brain obvious to hopefully only myself.

It was a success, showing what a small group of people can do with a clear focus. Local artists, crafters and organic growers displayed wares, cheese-makers and worm farmers gave demonstrations. Families lounged on bales of hay enjoying the talents of a line-up of musicians. Youngsters loved to draw, make masks, delighting in the mysterious appearance of the story teller dressed in black and purple Celtic attire to tell her riveting children's story. A favourite was music making with a teacher who knew how to bring out the inner muse. What was missing from this peaceful event was the raucous noise of rowdy people who have forgotten the art of living as a family and community. Moneymaking was missing as it did not take a focus, the small entry fee going towards future costs, no charge to stall holders and time freely given by many. Drumming drew all age groups to reconnect a primal cord attached to a forgotten way of life. It was a day of celebration.

When pondering on the event, I realised that I had survived an ordeal that could have been a soul destroying or a soul blessing experience and that too is celebration. There was still a way to go to rebuild strength and vitality from the cancer, the treatments and the shock to the body. However, twelve months earlier when lying in a hospital bed cradled in white sheets, surrounded by peeping technology and hooked up to machines, a 'then goal' was to be part of the next festival. I have done just that.

Diana was there to support in putting together the programme, Derek made a camp fire out of sticks on which hung a billy to sit under the storytelling tree. Lee made the long trek up the mountain to witness my remarkable fete and others supported in ways they never knew.

Taking small steps is a key to restoring health. Support is a big key. I believe the main ingredients to include in the wellness cake to be baked are love, support, nurturing and someone to celebrate your journey. This is a life-changing experience and it can be so for anyone wishing to be a part. Although they may see the obvious loss of weight, hair, vitality and strength, such a person will also glimpse an inner light that perhaps is now shining a little brighter. *"An aged man is but a paltry thing, a tattered coat upon a stick, unless soul clap its hands and sing ..."* wrote William Butler Yeats in his famous poem, *Sailing to Byzantium* (Schmidt, 2006).

For those who love a person doing a cancer journey, embark on that trip up the mountain to be a silent witness. Make the time to see the small steps taken, listen to what is said beneath the angst and be interested in the treatment programme. Above all, although your input is important, never impose what you think is right for them. Twelve months on from those life-fighting memories, having someone say, "Well done," whether in words, a smile or a knowing hug is the Oscar received for an award-winning performance. This is not an "It's over now, you're alright mate," process as threads are being woven into a new blanket in the making. Respect the fact that they may not want to be a part of the 'old partying ways' or talk on the 'phone for hours listening to details about Uncle Fred's long-ago departure, again! Whether for a short time or for the rest of their life, an inner journey has been embarked upon where silence is golden and the soul can dance and sing.

That is celebration.

When I first became ill, which was approximately six years ago, there was a weakening of the right side of my body and a reduced use of my right arm. That trickster hiding in my right breast was not within conscious awareness at the time and no doubt, was having a lovely time feeding off my life force. A massage therapist who can accurately read the body and not only remove lumps and bumps but can bring back alignment, restored that side of my body to normal. Toxins from physical, emotional and mental stress lingering in pockets of flesh are gently released by this man who truly walks his heart-felt ideals.

This was not a therapy I could have during the chemotherapy and operation process however, it is a valuable tool to realign the body and remove built-up tension. At the end of my first session with him following the aftermath of chemotherapy and the surgery, he commented that he had seen a lot of women who had undergone a similar ordeal but rarely one whose body had the calm and peace I portrayed at that time.

I take this as confirmation that by following the promptings of the inner witness, taking hold of the reigns and guiding those horses my way, the process I embarked on was the best for my own wellbeing. That too is celebration!

It Is What It Is

I had lunch with Lee this week and she said, "Ruchi, you're laughing again."

It is now two-and-a-half years since my diagnosis, however, it is much longer since the beginning of the journey. I can clearly see that I was like an orchestra playing with 'out of tune' instruments, representing people and events in my life that were draining my energy. With the inevitable crescendo, my life fell apart. My thinking was that I would pick up the pieces and keep going regardless. As I have always done, I put on a smile and spent the next two years studying and building onto a previously laid foundation for a new way of life. However, this did not come about in the way I had thought, as I then found myself 'on the floor', devoid of energy. The cords attached to unhealthy situations had snapped and I had no awareness of what had happened.

The practitioner I was seeing at the time believed the poisoning used to eradicate white ants from my home was the last straw. I am sure that it was but perhaps this came as a disguised gift because there were many notes in the opus I had written that were out of tune. It was time to hear my soul's song and in the years to follow, I learnt to let go of almost everything in my life, to stand naked and unafraid. How could I have come to know hope if I had not experienced despair? How could I have come to know the true value of health if I had not experienced disease?

Tears of grief wash away old toxic debris and I learnt to let them flow through me, releasing and purging. When I said to the acupuncturist, that sometimes I still cried, he replied that I had been through a world war three and had survived. Like a person suffering from post-traumatic stress disorder, this was the aftermath, but now it was coming from a place of healing and not illness. This gave me an understanding of how long it takes to rebuild on many levels from cancer and treatments such as chemotherapy. When telling this to Nalani, she replied that a relative of hers had experienced chemotherapy and when this lady cried, the family cried with her for as long as it took. In our Western culture, being busy is what we do which is vastly different from the Solomon Islands' way. "Get over it," is a message often given by words, looks or an impatient gesture. "Take this pill," a practitioner might say. Perhaps all we have to do is mirror the moment and be with whatever that brings.

Instead of fighting to 'make things right' I believe I now have an awareness of allowing the waves of life to flow through me. My concept of 'right' or 'wrong' is an illusion, a conditioning of my upbringing and society's agenda. The song is written, all I have to do is dance.

It is what it is, Aron says.

I Have A Vision

Five-and-a-half years ago, the words, "You have cancer," changed my life and with trepidation I stepped onto what I call the highway of hope in order to achieve the health I enjoy today.

I now know that cancer is not such a hit and miss affair. Laboratories around the world can now carry out a test to track the circulating tumour cells (CTC), the ones that cause metastases. Lifestyle changes and therapies to bring a return to health can be monitored to see if they are working. A blood test can indicate what supplements, herbs and foods will support your efforts and what chemotherapy will work best for your particular cancer. In *My Angry Breast*, you have glimpsed the work of doctors and scientists who are leading the way to an integrative approach and there are many who courageously walk this new path.

I glimpse a future world where clean food (organic, grown in season in healthy soil) will be considered the highest medicine, together with a lifestyle echoing the wisdom of the ancestors. Breathing clean air, walking barefoot on the earth and understanding the words of the old Slovakian proverb, "Pure water is the world's first and foremost medicine."

I glimpse technology that will promote healing by realigning the body with waves of sound and light. The practitioners of the future will have an understanding of the bodies of man and how they interact.

I glimpse a future where all peoples come together to build communities made from the building blocks of supportive and loving family units.

I have a vision that I believe is in the consciousness of today's peoples.

I recently had a breast massage, a wonderful therapy for women who have had breast surgery and indeed, an excellent preventative tool. The therapist commented on how peaceful my breast area is and this, she said, was due to the work I had done. Yes, I have worked hard on all levels of my being and I also have the gift of a wonderful integrative doctor whose skills and knowledge align with the new emerging medical paradigm. My Vision Boat has reached a safe harbour, its crew holding tried and true. My precious boys, Deb, grandchildren and friends have weathered the storms and navigated the waves.

The journey began with my doctor's words, "That's an angry breast," and at the end of the session the massage therapist's words, "That's not an angry breast," were a sign that it is now my time to begin a new dream.

I thank you, the reader, for sharing my journey. Love and blessings go with you on yours.

Reference List

Adams, M. (2017) *The Truth About Vaccines*, Documentary Mini-Series, 12-19 April (online) available at: www.thetruthaboutvaccines.com (accessed: 19.4.2017).

Aihara, H. (1986) *Acid & Alkaline*, 5th edn, California: George Ohsawa Macrobiotic Foundation.

Almeida, D. J. de, Bennemann, G.D., Bianchi, C.C. and Freitas, G.B.L. de (2014) *Colourful, Cute, Attractive and Carcinogenic: The Dangers of Dyes*, Cancer Research Journal, Vol. 2, No. 6-1, pp. 42-48.

Batmanghelidj, F. (2008) *Your Body's Many Cries for Water*, 3rd edn, USA: Global Health Solutions, Inc.

BioInitiative 2012 - *A Rationale for Biologically-Based Exposure Standards for Low-intensity Electromagnetic Radiation*, (online) available at www. bioinitiative.org. (accessed: 20.2.2013).

Braden, G. (2008) *The Spontaneous Healing of Belief*, Hay House Australia Pty Ltd.

Braden, G. (2009) *Fractal Time*, Hay House Australia Pty Ltd.

Brogan, K. (n.d.) "*Celebrating Dr Nicholas Gonzalez, A Legend In His Time*" (online) available at www.kellybroganmd.com/celebrating-dr-nicholas-gonzalez-legend-time (accessed: 3.6.2016).

Bryant, W. (1993) *The Veiled Pulse of Time: Life Cycles and Destiny (Spirituality and Social Renewal)*, New York: Lindisfarne Press.

Buckley, B. (2010) *Transition Farms*, Mount Tamborine: Castelen Press.

Buckley, G. (2008) *Growing Healthy*, Mount Tamborine: Castelen Press.

Cherry, N. (2001) *Evidence that Electromagnetic fields from high voltage powerlines and in buildings, are hazardous to human health, especially to young children*, (online) available at www.neilcherry.nz/document-downloads.html (accessed: 4.6.2015).

Cherry, N. (2002) *Actual or potential effects of ELF and RF/MW radiation on enhancing violence and homicide, and accelerating aging of human, animal or plant cells*, (online) available at www.neilcherry.nz/document-downloads.html (accessed: 8.6.2015).

Chopra, D. (2006) *Power Freedom and Grace*, California: Amber-Allen Publishing Inc.

Cilento, R. (1993) *Heal Cancer*, Melbourne: Hill of Content Publishing Company Pty Ltd.

Clark, H. R. (1993) *The Cure for all Cancers*, Chula Vista: New Century Press.

Colmsjo, M. (2009) *Sugar Dreams - Waking up to the Bitter Reality*, Australia.

Connett, P., Beck, J. and Micklem, H. (2010) *The Case Against Fluoride*, White River Junction: Chelsea Green Publishing Company.

Consolo, C. (2013) *Nuked Radio Special: Nuked in the Skies: celebrity sickness and flying, Part 1*, Interview with Leuren Moret, 25 March, (video file) available at www.youtube.com/watch?v=i_tRTBkul5I (accessed: 30.6.2013).

Contreras, E. (2013) *The Contreras Metabolic Integrative Therapy*, (online) The Cure To Cancer Summit, 18-28 September, available at www.thecuretocancersummit.com/schedule (accessed: 19.9.2013).

Cousins, G. (2014) *Blessing Water*, (online) available at www treeoflifecenterus.com/blessing-water (accessed: 15.3.2016).

Crook, P. (2014) *Just Be Quiet*, North Tamborine: Peter Crook.

Davis, D. (2007) *The Secret History of the War on Cancer*, Philadelphia: Perseus Books Group.

Druda, A. (2009) *The Tao of Rejuvenation*, California: Dharma Café Books and North Atlantic Books.

Duke Today (2002) *Duke Pharmacologist Says Animal Studies on DEET's Brain Effects Warrant Further Testing*, (online) available at www. today.duke.edu/2002/05/deet0502 (accessed: 27.7.2013).

Dupree U. (2012) *Ho'oponopono*, Scotland: Earthdancer.

Electromagnetic Health.org (2011) *The Seletun Scientific Statement*, (online) Media Advisory by Emily, available at www.electromagnetichealth.org/ electromagnetic-health-blog/the-seletun-statement (accessed: 6.8.2014).

Electromagnetic Health.org (2012) *The Russian National Committee on Non-Ionizing Radiation Protection Will Issue a Report Calling for Caution Based on 50 Years of EMF Research*, (online) Press Release by Emily, available at www.electromagnetichealth.org/electromagnetic-health-blog/rncnrp-report (accessed: 11.06.2014).

Ellwood, P., Asher, M.I., Garcia-Marcos, L., Williams, H., Keil, U., Robertson, C., Nagel, G. and ISAAC Phase III Study Group (2013) *Do fast foods cause asthma, rhinoconjunctivitis and eczema? Global findings from the International Allergies in Childhood (ISAAC) Phase Three.* Thorax April; 68(4):351-60.

Emerson, Ralph Waldo, BrainyQuote.com, Xplore Inc, 2017, available at: https://www.brainyquote.com/quotes/quotes/r/ralphwaldo101322.html, (accessed 12.5.2017).

Emoto, M. (2003) *The True Power of Water*, New York: Atria Books.

Epstein, S. (2013) *Stop Breast Cancer Before It Starts*, New York: Seven Stories Press.

Evans, M. and Rodger, I. (2000) *Healing for Body, Soul and Spirit*, Edinburgh: Floris Books.

Fang, M.D., Fall, K., Mittleman, M.A., Sparén, P.H., Ye, W., Adami, H-O. and Valdimarsdóttir, U. (2012) *Suicide and Cardiovascular Death after a Cancer Diagnosis*, N Engl J Med 366:1310-1318.

Farrow, L. (2013) *The Iodine Crisis: What You Don't Know About Iodine Can Wreck Your Life*, New York: Devon Press.

Fischer, W. (2000) *How to Fight Cancer and Win*, Toorak: Bookman Health.

Fisher, D. (2009) *More Silent Fields: Cancer and the Dirty Electricity Plague*, Buddina: Joshua Books.

Fortson, L. (2011) *Embrace, Release, Heal*, Boulder: Sounds True, Inc.

Fox, S. (1991) *Perspectives on Human Biology*, Dubuque: Wm. C. Brown Publishers.

Frankl, V. (2006) *Man's Search for Meaning*, 5th edn, Massachusetts: Beacon Press (First published in Germany in 1946).

Gerson, C. and Bishop, B. (2010) *Healing the Gerson Way*, 4th edn, California: Gerson Health Media.

Gerson, C. and Walker, M. (2006) *The Gerson Therapy*, 2nd edn, New York: Kensington Publishing Group.

Gerson, M. (2002) *A Cancer Therapy of Fifty Cases and The Cure of Advanced Cancer by Diet Therapy: A Summary of Thirty Years of Clinical Experimentation*, San Diego: Gerson Institute.

Gotzsche, P. (2011) *Mammography screening ten years on: reflections on a decade since the 2001 review*, (online) available at www.community-archive.cochrane.org/news/blog/mammography-screening-ten-years-reflections-decade-2001-review (accessed: 9.12.2012).

Greenberg, E. (2007) *Practical Solutions for Autism Recovery*, Explore! for the Professional, Vol. 16, No. 4, (online) available at: www.klinghardtinstitute.com/articles/ (accessed: 2.7.2015).

Griffin, E. (1997) *World Without Cancer*, 2nd edn. Westlake Village, California: American Media.

Grossman, E. (2009) *Chasing Molecules*, Washington, D.C.: Island Press.

Guthrie, K.S. (Discovered and Translated) (1998) *Second Book of Acts*, New Zealand: John Whitman Ray Publications.

Haley, B. (n.d.) *The Relationship of the Toxic Effects of Mercury to Exacerbation of the Medical Condition classified as Alzheimer's Disease*, Report to FDA, (on line) available at www.vce.org/mercury/haley-fda.pdf (accessed 28.3.2017).

Haley, B. (2005) *Mercury toxicity: Genetic susceptibility and synergistic effects*, Medical Veritas 2, 535-542.

Hall, D. (1976) *The Natural Health Book*, Victoria: Thomas Nelson Australia.

Helbig, K. (2010) *Patients die in agony because difficult words remain unsaid, says top surgeon,* (online), Courier Mail, available at www.couriermail.com.au/lifestyle/health/patients-die-in-agony-because-difficult-words-remain-unsaid-says-top-surgeon/story-e6frer7f-1225936837797.

Heyes, J.D. (2011) *Fukashima Orders of Magnitude Worse Than Chernobyl Says Dr Caldicott,* (online) available at www.naturalnews.com/032411_Fukashima_Chernobyl.html (accessed: 3.6.2013).

Ho, M.-W. (2013) *The New Genetics and Natural Versus Artificial Genetic Modification,* Entropy, 15(11), 4748-4781.

Howe, L. M. (2000) *British Cell Phone Safety Alert and An Interview with Robert O Becker, M.D.,* (online) available at: www.energyfields.org/science/becker.html. (accessed: 3.7.2015).

Huggins, H. (2010) *DNA Studies Confirm Dr Western Price's Century-old Findings,* (online) available at www.westernaprice.org/holistic-healthcare/root-canal-dangers (accessed: 3 3.2016).

Huggins, H. (n.d.) *Hal Huggin's Quotes,* (on line) available at: www.azquotes.com/author/48396-Hal_Huggins (accessed: 6.4.2017).

Hunter, B.T. (2011) *Our Toxic Legacy,* Laguna Beach: Basic Health Publications, Inc.

IFOF, Prod. (2012) *Yet We Sow: Voices of Organic Farmers After Fukashima,* (video file) available at www.youtube.com/watch?v=MPd7YPtiwo (accessed: 5.7.2013).

Jimenez, T. (2015) *Cancer Causing Blindspots, Toxic Vaccines, Homeopathy and the Power of Emotions,* The Truth About Cancer: A Global Quest Transcripts p 160, USA, TTAC Publishing.

Kaufman, C. S., Jacobson, L. Bachman, B.A., Kaufman, L.B. (2006) *Digital documentation of the physical examination: moving clinical breast exam to the electronic mechanical record*, Am J of Surg. Oct; 192(4):444-9.

Kaiser Permanente, Division of Research (2011) *Study Finds Exposure to Magnetic Fields in Pregnancy Increases Asthma Risk*, (online) News Release, available at: www.dor.kaiser.org/...Study_Finds_Exposure_to_Magnetic_Fields_in_Pregnancy_Increases_Asthma_Risk (accessed: 4.7.2014).

Kennedy, R.F. Jr. (n.d.) *Mercury is Not Safe in Any Form: Debunking the Myths About Thimerosal "Safety"*, (online) available at: http://worldmercuryproject.org/thimerosal-history/thimerosal-faq/ (accessed: 16.7.2017).

Kimbrell, A. (2007) *Your Right to Know*, San Rafael: Earth Aware Editions.

Kushi, K. (1991) *Macrobiotics and Oriental Medicine*, Tokyo and New York: Japan Publications Inc.

Lai, H., Sasaki, T. and Singh, N.P. (2005) *Targeted treatment of cancer with artemisinin and artemisinin-tagged iron-carrying compounds*, October 9(5):995-1007.

Lamech, F. (2014) *Self-reporting of symptom development from exposure to radiofrequency fields of wireless smart meters in Victoria, Australia: a case series*. Altern Ther Health Med. Nov-Dec;20(6): 28-39.

Lev, E., and Amar, Z., (2008) *Practical Materia Medica of the Medieval Eastern Mediterranean According to the Cairo Genizah*, Leiden, Boston: Brill (on line) available at www.t27.ir/Files/121/Library/3211273a-0c4d-4c04-8ca4-589d5ef9c928.pdf (accessed: 6.4.2017).

Levitt, B. Blake, (2007) *Electromagnetic Fields - a consumer's guide to the issues and how to protect ourselves,* An Authors Guild Backinprint. com Edition, Lincoln: iUniverse, Inc.

Lipton, B. (2005) *The Biology of Belief,* Alexandria: Hay House Australia Ltd.

Manikkam, M., Tracey, R., Guerrero-Bosagna, C. and Skinner, M.K. (2012) *Pesticide and Insect Repellent Mixture (Permethrin and DEET) Induces Epigenetic Transgenerational Inheritance of Disease and Sperm Epimutations,* Reprod Toxicol Dec;34(4):708-19.

Mauro, I. (2013) *A Conversation with Vandana Shiva - Question 6 - Seeds as the spinning wheel of today,* (video file) available at www.youtube. com/watch?v=Ub2rvFi0k_w (accessed: 3.7.2014).

Mazzucco, M. Dir, (2010) *Cancer The Forbidden Cures,* Italy: Top Documentary Films.

McDonald, J. and Janz, S. (Author.) 2017, *The Acupuncture Evidence Project: A Comparative Literature Review,* Revised, Australian Acupuncture & Chinese Medicine Association Ltd, Coorparoo.

McDonald-Smith, J. (2011) *How to Save the Planet from Your Bathtub,* Australia.

Mercola, J. (2010) *Why Did the Russians Ban Microwave Appliances Found in 90% of Americans Homes,* (online) available at www.articles. mercola.com/sites/articles/archive.2010/05/18/microwave-hazards, (accessed: 10.11.2013).

Mercola, J. (2011) *Sudden Death Syndrome: The Hidden Epidemic Destroying Your Gut Flora,* (online) available at www.articles.mercola. com/...2011/12/10/dr-don-huber-interview-part-1 (accessed: 1.2.2014).

MOA International (2006) *Working To Build Healthy Families, Working For a Better Future,* (first Japanese edition: 1 January, 2006) Japan: MOA International.

Moalem, S. (2008) *Survival of the Sickest,* London: Harper Collins Publishers.

Monte, W. (n.d.) *Dangers of Aspartame,* (online) available at www.whilesciencesleeps.com/dangers-of-aspartame (accessed: 29.3.2013).

Morgan, G., Ward, R. and Barton, M. (2004) *The contribution of cytotoxic chemotherapy to 5-year survival in adult malignancies,* Clin Oncol (R Coll Radiol) Dec; 16(8):549-60.

Nahmad, C. (2008) *Angel Healing,* London: Watkins Publishing.

Napoli, M. (2002) *Mammography: Should You Have One?* (online) available at www.medicalconsumers.org/article-archive (accessed: 4.1.2012).

Nelson, B. (2007) *The Emotion Code,* Mesquite: Wellness Unmasked Publishing.

Oberst, L. (2016) *Why India's First 100% Organic State Matters for the Future of Organic Food,* Food Revolution Network (online) available at www.foodrevolution.org/blog/organic-food-sikkim (accessed: 26.5.2016).

Okada, M. (2005) *Toward Families Filled With Beauty,* Japan: MOA International. (First Japanese edition: November 1, 2004).

Pandey, S. (2015) *Human Clinical Trials on Cancer Killing Dandelion Extract,* (online) available at www.uwindsor.ca/dailynews/2015-02-18/human-clinical-trials-cancer-killing-dandelion-extract (accessed: 14.3.2016).

Perlmutter, D. (2017) *Stunning New Science on the Gut-Brain Connection*, Food Revolution Summit (on line) available at: www.foodrevolutionsummit.org (accessed: 5.5.2017).

Pesticide Action Network North America (2012) *A Generation In Jeopardy: how pesticides are undermining our children's health and intelligence*, (online) available at www.panna.org/resources/publication/-report/report-generation-in-jeopardy (accessed: 9.9.2013).

Plant, J. (2000) *Your Life In Your Hands*, London: Virgin Publishing Ltd.

Reid, D. (1993) *Guarding the Three Treasures*, London: Simon & Schuster Ltd.

Renter, E. (2013) *Second-largest Dutch City Bans Monsanto's Roundup Herbicide*, (online) available at www.naturalsociety.com/second-largest-dutch-city-bans-monsantos-roundup (accessed: 9.9.2013).

Rogers, S. (2002) *Detoxify or Die*, Sarasota: Sand Key Company Inc.

Rossetti, F. (1992) *Psycho-regression - A new system for healing and personal growth*, London: Judy Piatkus (Publishers) Ltd.

Rumi, J. (2004) *The Essential Rumi*, (Barks, C. with Nicholson, R., Arberry, A.J., Moyne, J., Trans), New York, Harper Collins (original work published in 1273).

Samsel, A. and Seneff, S. (2013) *Glyphosate's Suppression of Cytochrome P450 Enzymes and Amino Acid Biosynthesis by the Gut Microbiome: Pathways to Modern Disease*, Entropy, 15(4), 1416-1463.

Scarpa, E-S. and Ninfali, P. (2015) *Phytochemicals as Innovative Therapeutic Tools against Cancer Stem Cells*, Int. J. Mol. Sci. 16(7), 15727-15742.

Schmidt, M., ed., (2006) *The Great Modern Poets: Anthology of the Best Poets and Poetry 1900*, U.K.: Quercus Books.

Schweitzer, Albert, BrainyQuote.com, Xplore Inc, available at: www. brainyquote.com/quotes/quotes/a/albertschw161528.html (accessed 11.4.2017).

Sellman, S. (2003) *Mothers Prevent Your Daughters From Getting Breast Cancer*, USA, GetWell Foundation.

Séralini, G-E, Clair, E., Mesnage, R., Gress, S., Defarge, N., Malatesta, M., Hennequin, D. and Spiroux de Vendômois, S. (2014) *Republished study: long-term toxicity of a Roundup herbicide and a Roundup-tolerant genetically modified maize*, Environ. Sci. Eur., 26:14.

Sherwood, P. (2007) *Holistic Counselling a New Vision for Mental Health*, Bunbury: Sophia Publications.

Simpson, L. (2000) *The Healing Energies of Earth*, London: Gaia Books Limited.

Smith, J. (2007) *Genetic Roulette*, Carlton, Victoria: Gene Ethics.

Soffritti, M., Belpoggi, F., Degli-Esposti, D., Lambertini, L., Tibaldi, E. and Rigano, A., (2006) *First Experimental Demonstration of the Multipotential Carcinogenic Effects of Aspartame Administered in the Feed to Sprague-Dawley Rats*, Environ Health Perspect. Mar; 114(3): 379-385.

Spittle, B. (2008) *Fluoride Fatigue*, Dunedine: Paua Press Limited.

Vitale, J. (2007) *Zerolimits*, New Jersey: John Wiley & Sons, Inc.

Vrain, T. (2013) *Former Pro-GMO Scientist Speaks Out On The Real Dangers Of Genetically Modified Foods*, GMO Mini-Summit,

25-27 October, available at www.gmosummit.org/former-pro-gmo-scientist (accessed: 25.10.2013).

Walker, F. (2014) *Maralinga*, Sydney: Hatchette Australia.

Wallach, J., Lan, M. and Schrauzer, N. (2014) *Epigenetics: The Death of the Genetic Theory of Disease Transmission*, New York: SelectBooks, Inc.

Wolverton, B. C., Douglas, W. L. and Bounds, K. (1989) *A study of interior landscape plants for indoor air pollution abatement*, (online) available at www: archive.org/details/nasa_techdoc_19930072988 (accessed: 20.4.2016).

Yanagisawa, Dr Atsuo (n.d.) *Effect of Vitamin C and Antioxidative Nutrition on Radiation-induced Gene Expression in Fukashima Nuclear Plant Workers*, (online) Japanese College of IV Therapy, available at www.doctoryourself.com/Radiation_VitC.pptx.pdf (accessed: 2.7.2013).

Bibliography

Ausubel, K. (2000) *When Healing Becomes a Crime*, Vermont: Healing Arts Press.

Braden, G. (2007) *The Divine Matrix*, Hay House Australia Pty. Ltd.

Burrell, L. (2010) *Cell Phone Radiation Destroys Sleep and Threatens Immune System*, (online) available at www.electricsense.com/832/cell-phone-radiation-destroys-sleep-and-threatens-immune-system-3 (accessed: 4.6.2013).

Caldicott, H. (2006) *Nuclear Power Is Not The Answer*, Victoria: Melbourne University Press.

Chevallier, A. (1996) *Encyclopedia of Medicinal Plants*, St Leonards: DK Publishing.

Cole, S.W. (2014) *Human Social Genomics*, PLoS Genetics 10(8): e1004601. https://doi.org/10.1371/journal.pgen.1004601.

Ellis, K. (2013) *Shattering the Cancer Myth*, 4th edn. Australia: Ellis-Crawford Media (1st edn Hinkler Books 2003, 2nd edn Zeus Publications 2010, 3rd edn Ellis-Crawford Media).

Eversole, F. (2013) *Energy Medicine Technologies*, Vermont: Inner Traditions.

Fisher, D. (2008) *Silent Fields: The Growing Cancer Cluster Story*, Karragarra Island: Lindlahr Book Publishing.

Green, M. (1997) *Exploring the World of the Druids*, London: Thomas & Hudson Ltd.

Kennedy, R.F., Jr., (2015) *Thimerosal - Let The Science Speak*, New York: Skyhorse Publishing.

Lam, M. (2004) *Artemisinin (Wormwood) - From Malaria to Cancer*, (online) available at www.drlam.com/blog/artemisinin-wormwood-from-maleria-to-cancer/405 (accessed: 3.8.2014).

Murray, M. and Pizzorna, J. (2012) *The Encyclopedia of Natural Medicine*, 3rd edn, New York: Atria, A Division of Simon & Schuster, Inc.

Paull, J. (2007) *Trophobiosis Theory: A Pest Starves On a Healthy Plant*, Elementals Journal of Bio-Dynamics, Tasmania, 88:24, archived at www.orgprints.org/12894/1/12894.pdf.

Pierce, T.H. (2009) *Outsmart Your Cancer*, 2nd edn, Nevada: Thoughtworks Publishing.

Pratt, S. and Matthew, K. (2004) *Super Foods*, Sydney: Random House Australia (Pty. Ltd.).

Reader's Digest, (1994) *Magic and Medicine of Plants*, Surry Hills: Reader's Digest (Australia) Pty Limited.

Reid, D. (1998) *Chi-Gung, Harnessing the Power of the Universe*, London: Simon & Schuster Ltd.

Reid, D. (n.d.) *Electromagnetic Energy Pollution*, (on line) available at www.danreid.org/daniel-reid-articles-electro-magnetic-energy-pollution.asp.

Sayer, J. (2012), *Crouching Garnish, Hidden Superfood: The Secret Life of Kale*, (online) available at www.greenmedinfo.com/blog/crouching-garnish-hidden-superfood-secret-life-kale (accessed: 22.9.2013).

Shinrin-Yoku: The Medicine of Being in the Forest, (online) available at www.shinrin-yoku.org (accessed: 12.3.2015).

Sircus, M. (2013) *Pure Water*, (online) available at www.drsircus.com/medicine/water/pure-water (accessed: 3.8.2013).

Smith, J. (2003) *Seeds of Deception*, Australia: Scribe Publications.

Smith, R. and Lourie, B. (2009) *Slow Death by Rubber Duck*, St Lucia: University of Queensland Press.

Statham, Bill and Schneider, L. (2006) *The Chemical Maze*, Australia: Possibility.Com.

Swerdlow, J. *Nature's Medicine, Plants That Heal*, Washington: National Geographic Society.

Szasz, A. (2007) *Shopping Our Way to Safety*, Minneapolis: University of Minnesota Press.

University of California San Francisco Publication (1994) *Gofman on the Health Effects of Radiation: There Is No Safe Threshold*, Volume 38, Number 16, Page 20.

Vanderheyden, S. and Fritz, H. (2014) *Mistletoe Therapy*, (online) available at www.ihpmagazine.com/mistletoe-therapy (accessed: 4.1.2014).

Wallace, H. (2011) *Finding Wellness, Success and Health*, Ormeau, Australia.

Wright, J. (2001) *Reflexology and Acupuncture*, London: Chancellor Press.

Index

A

B

C

H

I

J

K

L

M

N

O

P

Q

R

S

"Out beyond ideas of wrongdoing
and rightdoing there is a field.
I'll meet you there."

Jalal-ad-Din Rumi (2004, p 36)

About the Author

Ruchi, a teacher of yoga, holistic counsellor, psychological astrologer and a story teller attributes her success in navigating the cancer labyrinth to many factors. Her passion for research into the field of health, seeded when witnessing her father's cancer experience and the body/mind/spirit teachings acquired during the years of becoming a teacher. Ruchi believes that combining traditional and natural therapies, working with a supportive team, maintaining a healthy diet and lifestyle regime and listening to her inner guidance are crucial to the journey.

My Angry Breast is based on a real-life story expressed through Ruchi's love for words and for walking softly on our Earth so as to create a healthy, peaceful and loving experience.

Printed in the United States
By Bookmasters